Nuclear War in the UK

If Britain is attacked by nuclear bombs or by missiles, we do not know what targets will be chosen or how severe the assault will be.

If nuclear weapons are used on a large scale, those of us living in the country areas might be exposed to as great a risk as those in the towns. The radioactive dust, falling where the wind blows it, will bring the most widespread dangers of all. No part of the United Kingdom can be considered safer than another.

The dangers which you and your family will face in this situation can be reduced if you do as this booklet describes.

Nuclear War in the UK

Taras Young

Four Corners Irregulars
N° 7

CHECK

All 3 projectiles

MUST fire and

burst in the air

Previous page: Introduction from *Protect and Survive* (1976).

Above: A page from Post Personnel Training Scheme materials prepared for the Royal Observer Corps (1989).

Contents

PROTECT&
SURVIVE
MONTHLY
& BRITISH/US.Civil Defence News

No.11   NOVEMBER 1981   65p $2

your guide to
surviving a
nuclear war

DO-IT-YOURSELF
Cellar Shelter
see page 12

Introduction

Defensive relics are scattered across the British landscape – from centuries-old hillforts and castles to Second World War pillboxes on hillsides; gun emplacements on estuary islands, creaking sea forts, and concrete anti-tank cubes that litter rivers and fields. Look more closely and you might spot some newer additions – military radio masts, abandoned missile stores, towering, windowless telephone exchanges, and the surface-level signs of nuclear bunkers.

During the Cold War, in parallel with these physical measures, successive British governments generated masses of official publications in preparation for a nuclear attack that never came. Like the radar stations and airfields and bunkers, these artefacts were there if you knew where to look, or how to see them – but you had to want to find them.

Nuclear war, with its unthinkable death, destruction and threat of societal collapse, doesn't really lend itself to sensible advice or practical guidance. Almost uniformly stoic and reserved, official public information issued by central government rationalised the horror of nuclear holocaust into a calming blandness – except where it occasionally suited their needs to bring fear to the fore. Sometimes, government advice appears quaint and of-its-time, counterproductive or even foolish. But it's worth considering each of these artefacts beyond face value and questioning why they exist. Public information isn't created in a vacuum, and it's rarely designed solely to inform. Each piece of government literature, even where it's not overtly political, is a piece of propaganda; each has its own agenda bubbling below the surface; each was commissioned, written and designed by people who were knowingly playing a role in a wider political performance.

Some might find it difficult to overcome the overpowering dread and helplessness induced by reading about the threat of nuclear war. However, my intention in bringing so many of these documents together is not to fetishise or trivialise that reaction. Instead, this book seeks to tell the story of the British state trying to make sense of a universal threat. It presents a cross-section of official materials produced about nuclear attack by those whose job it was to instil in the British people a belief that there could be some defence. Behind these captivating documents were civil servants, council officials, scientists, copywriters, illustrators and designers working together to try to visualise a nation coping with an unimaginable horror – and then conveying those visions to the public in creative, authoritative and optimistic ways.

Like the defensive architecture that popped up all over the country, these documents were created by the institutions of government and hidden in plain sight. Quietly woven into the fabric of society, their existence went unnoticed and unquestioned by the majority of the public. Together they reveal the remarkable extent of the national preparations for a catastrophe that thankfully never happened.

Opposite: Last exit for Spaghetti Junction, as foreseen by the group Scientists Against Nuclear Arms (1982).

Next pages: The impact of an atomic strike, from *Today's Civil Defence* (early 1960s).

GROUND ZERO

the short-term effects of a nuclear attack on the West Midlands

80p

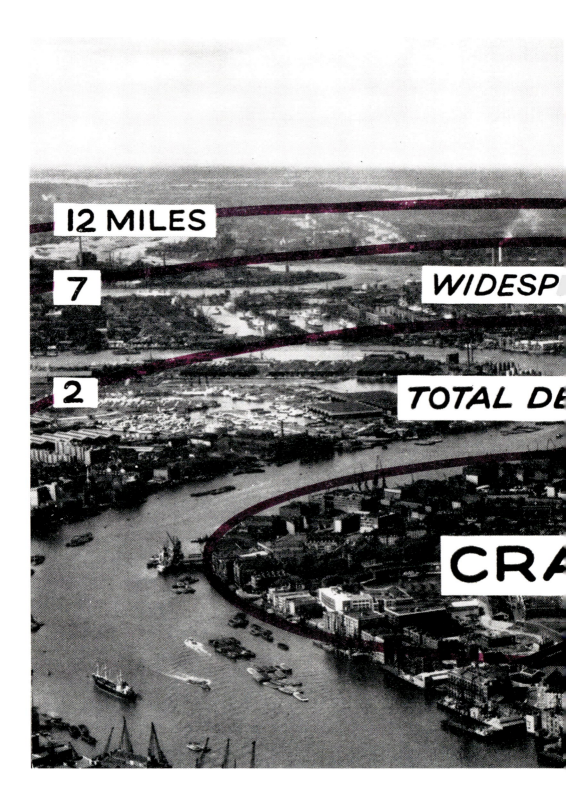

12 MILES

7

2

WIDESP

TOTAL DE

CRA

Informing the Public

Today, the idea of the government directly advising, informing and influencing the masses through instructional leaflets, posters and didactic TV ads seems of another age. Public information of this kind is an anachronism: gone, together with the paternalistic post-war state that helped it to thrive. However, the Cold War coincided with the heyday of public information. There were leaflets and posters and short films covering every aspect of life. At the heart of it all sat the Central Office of Information, the creative engine churning them out.

Founded in 1946 as a successor to the wartime Ministry of Information, the Central Office of Information (COI) was the government's in-house marketing and advertising agency – or, depending on your point of view, its peacetime propaganda unit. Their stated aim was to apply their communications expertise in a way that would help the government achieve its policy objectives. When a government department wanted to issue some advice to the public, inform them about a new initiative, or persuade them to think or act in a particular way, the COI was there to serve their needs. COI staff provided an end-to-end service, creating leaflets, booklets, posters, sound recordings and films on every topic under the sun, so long as it served the interests of the British government. Their work shaped and became embedded in the psyche of British society; it acquainted us with the NHS and decimal coinage; popularised characters such as the Green Cross Man; made public information films such as *Charley Says* and *Lonely Water* that affected whole generations, and advised people on everything from basic fire safety to AIDS and the Millennium Bug. On top of these well-known campaigns, the COI was commissioned to create much of the public information about the risks of nuclear attack.

Advice on the nuclear threat had its roots in air raid precautions leaflets produced during the Second World War, which advised not only what to do when an air raid took place, but what steps you could take to prepare for them. By following the guidance, Britons survived the Blitz. However, a much bigger threat was on its way.

The closing days of the war saw the development of the fission bomb, better known as the atomic bomb or A-bomb. This type of weapon caused the devastation at Hiroshima and Nagasaki. The destruction of whole cities was alarming, but the destruction wrought by the atomic bombs was viewed through the filter of similar indiscriminate attacks made possible through conventional weapons, such as carpet bombing. Early post-war advice on nuclear attack naturally drew on the recent experience of the Second World War, with references to respirators, incendiary bombs, and plans to build communal shelters. The public gained its first official guidance on the nuclear threat when the Home Office distributed a plain, four-page pamphlet in 1952, *Civil Defence and the Atom Bomb*. Providing little concrete advice and some dubious reassurance, it exposed a poor understanding of the bomb's impact. 'In the city of Hiroshima,' it said, 'over half the people within a mile from the explosion are still alive... contamination is not likely to last long.'

The illusion of relative safety was short-lived. That November, the US detonated a new kind of nuclear bomb: the first thermonuclear weapon, also known as the hydrogen or H-bomb. Using a combination of nuclear fusion and nuclear fission, there was the potential for the hydrogen bomb to be immensely more powerful than its predecessor. Britain unveiled its own H-bomb during the Grapple series of nuclear tests, which began in the spring of 1957. After three failed attempts to detonate a megaton weapon – which the government covered up – the first successful British detonation, Grapple X, took place in November that year. The shift in threat from A-bomb to H-bomb led to a corresponding shift in the tone of official advice. No longer able to pretend that a nuclear exchange wouldn't lay waste to much of the country, public information shed much of its 'Blitz spirit' optimism and instead began to focus on the practical measures people could take to prepare for the bomb. In 1957, as the vapour plumes of the Grapple tests grew and fell over the Indian Ocean, the Home Office released their most detailed public information about the Bomb yet.

The Hydrogen Bomb was published on 25 October 1957. A dark little booklet, it was illustrated in orange and black with line-drawn thermonuclear explosions, scenes of devastated city centres, and prim 1950s families taking shelter: under the stairs, in bunkers, in cellars, and – where none of those was available – sitting patiently in their living room. It laid out in some detail the technology and risks of the H-bomb, and what protective measures people could take. Within government, civil servants called the booklet 'a good effort', saying that it 'succeeds in the difficult

The Hydrogen Bomb

HER MAJESTY'S STATIONERY OFFICE

NINEPENCE NET

task of striking a balance between scientific exposition and any too facile 'penny dreadful' description of the hydrogen bomb.' It proved to be popular outside of government, too – wildly popular. Within three months, some 90,000 copies had been sold or distributed, and the official printers could hardly keep up. Members of the public wrote in to complain that they were struggling to find it at book stalls. Five years later, *The Hydrogen Bomb* was still the go-to advice: in February 1962, for instance, the Scottish Home Department wrote of their 'urgent requirement' that 70 copies be distributed to Church of Scotland ministers.

Behind the scenes, the Home Office was already preparing something different. An internal memo stated: 'The recent decision was not that the booklet *The Hydrogen Bomb* should be revised, but that something separate, shorter and cheaper should be produced in pamphlet form.' That pamphlet was *Advising the Householder on Protection against Nuclear Attack*, published in 1963. Starker both in its design and its message, and illustrated more profusely than its predecessor, the new booklet focused on practical, protective measures, actions to take during attack, and how to cope afterwards. This time, the government was prepared for the booklet to be popular, printing 500,000 copies, priced at ninepence each.

A slit trench with earth covering protects against blast and radiation

Previous page, above and opposite: *The Hydrogen Bomb* (1957).

However, it almost immediately came in for criticism from all quarters. A parliamentary committee slammed *Advising the Householder*, recommending it be withdrawn, saying it did not serve 'any useful purpose' and gave 'entirely the wrong impression' of Civil Defence preparations. Journalist Bernard Levin lambasted the booklet on the BBC's hugely popular satirical television show *That Was the Week That Was*. A pharmacist wrote in to complain that the booklet's first aid kit mistakenly included baking powder, rather than baking soda, which could have serious consequences if applied to skin burns or eyes. The booklet even made an appearance as a grim prop in Peter Watkins's harrowing pseudo-documentary, *The War Game*, in 1965, which the BBC barred from the airwaves as 'too horrifying for the medium of broadcasting'.

Remarkably, *Advising the Householder* remained the last official booklet on nuclear attack that the British government made generally available until the publication of *Protect and Survive* in 1980.

Early in 1955, the government tasked a committee, led by Sir William Strath, to determine how badly Britain would suffer in a nuclear conflict. The culmination of the committee's work, the Strath Report, painted a pessimistic picture: millions dead; millions more sick with radiation poisoning; industry, farming and cities in ruins, the United Kingdom on the brink of collapse. Following the Strath Report, and with the lessons of the Second World War still relatively fresh in mind, the British government began to take Civil Defence more seriously. This led to the publication of the 1957 *Hydrogen Bomb* pamphlet, but also to new plans for evacuation and dispersal.

In a rather unfortunate choice of terminology, government reports stated that they expected many people would 'self-evacuate' immediately following nuclear attack. The *Advising the Householder* pamphlet indicated that those people who found themselves in Z-Zones – areas of very heavy fall-out – would be advised by officials to pack their bags and drive to safer areas, giving their neighbours a lift where needed. A secret government briefing at the time said that the public would be educated in the lead-up to war to put 'lives before luggage', and that 'leaving a Z-Zone with an empty seat is a crime'. Complementing the expectation of self-evacuation were plans for the organised evacuation of vulnerable people. This was known as the Dispersal Scheme, and it was given considerable additional impetus by the fears generated by the Cuban Missile Crisis.

Indoor and outdoor shelters, from *Advising the Householder on Protection against Nuclear Attack* (1963).

SHELTER "CORES"

Outdoor Fall-out Shelter

If it is impossible for you to prepare an indoor fall-out shelter, a trench dug outside your home would provide good protection. It should be deep enough to provide comfortable standing room and the sides should be shored up. After placing supports across the trench, cover the top with boards, metal sheets or concrete slabs, and heap earth on top. Leave a manhole-type entrance with a movable cover such as a dustbin lid. Keep a small ladder or a pair of household steps there.

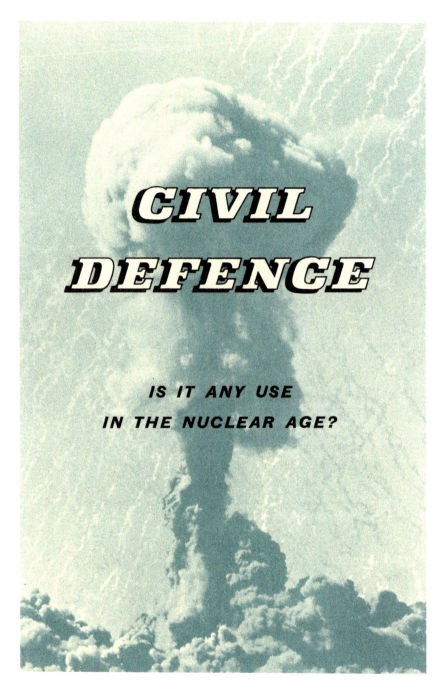

CIVIL DEFENCE

IS IT ANY USE
IN THE NUCLEAR AGE?

As well as material informing the public about nuclear attack,
the government also produced leaflets defending the national investment
in Civil Defence, and encouraging people to volunteer their time.

"All right,"
you may say,

"but suppose it never happens? Surely it's all so horrible it never **COULD** happen".

Let's hope you're right. This country is doing all it can to prevent war. But the choice might not be ours.

There is nothing sinister about Civil Defence, any more than there is about a peace-time Navy, Army or Air Force. Civil Defence is an essential part of our ordinary national preparedness.

But that doesn't mean that training in Civil Defence is useless in peace time.

DEFENCE REGULATIONS

IMPORTANT ANNOUNCEMENT

BILLETING

The Government have announced that the dispersal of people in priority classes from certain large towns shall be put into effect immediately.

The area covered by the..Council is a reception area* to which some of these people are being brought.

Occupiers of housing property in this area are required by law to provide accommodation for any persons assigned to them by the Billeting Officer. Every effort will be made to spread the burden of billeting fairly and equally between households.

It may be necessary to carry out billeting at night as well as day-time. Your co-operation in this emergency is requested.

An allowance will be paid to occupiers for the accommodation pro-vided. To claim this you will need a billeting allowance order form. Watch the bottom of this notice for further information about how to obtain the form.

CLERK OF THE COUNCIL

*If only part of the area is scheduled as a reception area, the districts affected are shown below:

Instructions for obtaining billeting allowance order form:

(86827–1) Wt. 39945/6387 100M 1/64 Hw.

Ministry of Housing and Local Government

DISPERSAL TRAVEL PASS

DAY

....(NAME)
is a member of the priority classes

Report to...

on..
....at............a.m./p.m.

Issuing authority..
....

Mcr. (7577)

Posters, leaflets and travel passes were produced to aid in evacuating
people if the Dispersal Scheme was ever activated (1964).

Materials to support the Dispersal Scheme, including posters, leaflets and travel passes, were printed in 1964. Evacuees would be drawn from those living in target areas – those in the 'priority classes': pregnant women; children, accompanied by their mothers or guardians (unless they had left school), and any disabled or elderly people. It is worth noting that this latter group was only eligible for evacuation if their carer was already leaving; the priority classes were therefore largely made up of those who might be considered 'young and able'. After arriving at their local dispersal centre, prospective evacuees would be issued with a travel pass, then return home to pack. They would assemble at an appointed time for transport by bus or train to the supposed safety of a predetermined 'reception area' in another part of the country. In the reception areas, volunteers would survey households to ascertain how many spare rooms were available, and whether they were prepared to take in unaccompanied children.

However, the Dispersal Scheme didn't last. The government's reassessment of Civil Defence in 1966 said it would be 'reviewed'; hindered further by the refusal of some left-leaning councils to play along, plans for mass evacuation of the British public were essentially shelved the following year. In the absence of an official evacuation scheme, the advice became to 'stay put'. This was backed by a belief within government that a European war would rapidly escalate to a full nuclear exchange, in which no part of the densely-populated country would be safe. The 'stay put' message was subsequently reinforced in *Protect and Survive*, which stated: 'If you leave, your local authority may need to take your empty house for others to use. So stay at home.'

In the early 1980s, the government began to reconsider their position on planned evacuation. In part, this was down to growing public scepticism of the 'stay put' policy – and its marked contrast with by then not-so-secret plans to evacuate ministers to the safety of government bunkers. It was also a reflection of the government's changed view that Soviet targeting would be more selective than previously held, leaving some parts of the country less at-risk to nuclear attack than others. A secret 1981 psychological study for the Home Office predicted that one fifth of the population would self-evacuate if war was looming, with a further third taking part in government evacuation schemes, if they were offered. (However, if the build-up to war lasted too long, it was believed that evacuees would start making their way back home – even as others were leaving for safety.) Early in 1983, options for a new evacuation programme were drawn up and presented to ministers. Hand-drawn maps showed suggested 'evacuation flows' out of target areas – including more than a million people leaving both Glasgow and Liverpool for the surrounding regions, and 3,182,000 being dispersed from London to places as far away as Wales and Cornwall. A further 114,000 would be moved out of Suffolk, with its US air bases and Sizewell nuclear power station, to neighbouring Norfolk. However, it seems the plans for a new scheme were not taken any further.

By the early 1970s, the Home Office decided to try its hand again at issuing public information about nuclear attack. However, the Britain of 1973 was quite a different place to that of a decade earlier, when *Advising the Householder* had been published. Civil servants were keen to pursue an approach that was more in keeping with the times. To that end, they planned out a campaign that would be broadcast-led, with pre-recorded radio announcements and engaging, animated TV films, supported – almost incidentally, this time – by a booklet.

Titled *Protect and Survive*, it was planned along the lines of a large-scale advertising campaign. The public would be primed with some initial films and radio broadcasts during a 'low-level crisis' – defined as weeks to months before attack. These films offered key information such as what a nuclear explosion was, what warnings you would be given, and why it was important to stay at home; they explained how to use the booklet, and outlined the construction of a basic shelter. These messages would later be reinforced by a second set of films during the 'preparatory period', as the likelihood of attack increased, covering everything from how to provision your fallout room, to life under fallout conditions, 'sanitation discipline' and burials. They also advised that now was the time to start building your makeshift fallout shelter. When attack seemed likely – a period termed 'probable inevitability of war' – all the films and radio broadcasts would be played repeatedly. The booklet would act as an *aide memoire* for what people should already have learned from the broadcasts.

Early discussions between Home Office departments show that not everyone agreed a booklet was necessary at all. 'It is by no means certain that we are going to have a Householder's Booklet,' wrote an irritated J. F. D. Buttery of F6 Division, the Home Office's emergency planning section, to a Mr Rawles of the Public Relations Branch. 'I thought I had made it clear that a booklet of predominantly visual material was only a possibility, not a firm undertaking.' Despite this initial uncertainty, by the time plans were finalised a year later, a fully-formed booklet did exist. Unlike previous booklets, though, *Protect and Survive* was designed to drop onto doormats as part of the wider campaign, supported by ministerial announcements, the TV and radio broadcasts, and pull-out newspaper supplements. The campaign intended that the booklet should be issued at 'a relatively late stage in the crisis'; internal Home Office memos explicitly stated that there were no plans to release the booklet until absolutely necessary, 'because it needed to be seen in conjunction with the rest of the publicity package, and the Department did not want to alarm the public'.

Early versions of the *Protect and Survive* booklet were replete with clumsy choices that were excised before publication. The text as initially drafted emphasised the 'stay put' policy with a slightly sinister tone: 'You are better off in your own home – Stay in the area you know and where you are known – Only fools run away'. Meanwhile, the Central Office of Information expressed concern that a section titled 'Deaths' would worry people – so the content was left in, but the heading itself was removed. A drawing of a householder preparing his makeshift shelter showed a table covered with soft cushions – a refuge more akin to a children's sofa fort than a nuclear bunker. This was replaced with 'harder' items, such as boxes of books, in the final version. Many elements made it from the earliest sketches to final publication, though – including the stylised 'nuclear family' silhouetted on the booklet's cover, a protective white circle shielding them from black and orange fallout.

Rough cuts of the campaign videos were shown in the Central Office of Information's private cinema at the end of November 1975. The *Protect and Survive* films were produced by the animation house responsible for children's cartoon *Crystal Tipps and Alistair*, Richard Taylor Cartoon Films, who also became well-known for the iconic *Charley Says* public information films. Each film opened and closed with an animated version of the nuclear family symbol, accompanied by an eerie 'musical logo' composed by Roger Limb of the BBC Radiophonic Workshop; they were narrated with gravitas by actor Patrick Allen. With the films and radio tapes completed early in 1976, around 2,000 copies of the booklet were printed up and issued to chiefs of police and heads of local authorities. These were sent out with a letter making it clear that no further copies would be made available; while this was partly to keep things under wraps, in order to retain the campaign's impact if it were needed, there were also more prosaic reasons for not printing more copies. By this point, the campaign budget was, in the words of a civil servant, 'sailing close to the wind'. Having blown nearly £94,000 on films, radio tapes, and extensive market research and testing of the advice, just £2,020 remained for printing the booklets, with no more money forthcoming.

PROTECT AND SURVIVE

This booklet tells you how to make your home and your family as safe as possible under nuclear attack

Protect and Survive was printed in 1976 but only received limited distribution; public outcry led to it being published more widely, with slight amendments, in 1980.

The booklet itself depicted the effects of a nuclear attack, and demonstrated how an ordinary family could prepare their home by blocking windows and chimneys. In plain language and simple line drawings, it provided advice on constructing a simple lean-to shelter using three doors, weighed down with household items like books, suitcases and drawers full of earth. It gave instructions for cobbling together a 'survival kit', and for constructing an improvised toilet from a chair frame and a bucket. It described the warnings you would hear that meant it was time to take cover in your refuge, and what to do with the bodies when your family members died.

For the next few years, public awareness of *Protect and Survive* was limited, although it was never a particularly well-kept secret. The booklet made occasional appearances in press reports and discussions of civil defence, and elements were sometimes re-used by local authorities in their own cobbled-together civil defence publications. That changed at the beginning of 1980, when the government's least-public publicity campaign suddenly exploded into view. A series of articles in *The Times* about the state of Britain's civil defence preparedness shed light on the campaign, prominently featuring the booklet's cover. Soon afterwards, excerpts from the films were broadcast on prime-time television, in an episode of the BBC's *Panorama* documentary strand titled *If the Bomb Drops*, hosted by a youthful Jeremy Paxman. The press and public demanded more information about the plans, latching on to the non-publication of *Protect and Survive* as a particular issue. Giving in to the pressure, and despite reservations expressed by Home Office public relations officers, the government made some hasty revisions to the booklet, and published it.

The reaction was immediate, and killed any chances *Protect and Survive* had of being taken seriously. The intention had been that the booklet should play a supporting role to the government broadcasts and announcements in a time of international crisis. Published outside of this context, the booklet seemed at once sinister and quite pathetic. It quickly found itself on the receiving end of a series of barbed cultural responses. As well as making an appearance in Raymond Briggs's deeply affecting graphic novel *When the Wind Blows*, *Protect and Survive* was lampooned by the bright young faces of alternative comedy. In one episode of anarchic sitcom *The Young Ones*, a nuclear weapon lands in the kitchen, but fails to go off. Declaring 'I'm going upstairs to get the incredibly helpful and informative *Protect and Survive* manual,' hippie pessimist Neil is seen holding the booklet in one hand, and painting himself white with the other, 'to deflect the blast'.

A small number of printers' proofs were prepared of tabloid
and broadsheet versions of *Protect and Survive*, to have been published
in the press in the lead-up to a nuclear attack.

PROTECT AND SURVIVE

Issued by H.M. Government

How to make your home as safe as possible under nuclear attack. Read this with care and keep it handy. Your life and the lives of your family may depend on it.

If Britain is attacked by nuclear bombs or by missiles, we do not know what targets will be chosen or how severe the assault will be.
If nuclear weapons are used on a large scale, those of us living in the country areas might be exposed to as great a risk as those in the towns. The radioactive dust, falling where the wind blows it, will bring the most widespread dangers of all. No part of the United Kingdom can be considered safe from both the direct effects of the weapons and the resultant fall-out.
The dangers which you and your family will face in this situation can be reduced if you follow the advice on these pages.

1 Challenge to survival

Everything within a certain distance of a nuclear explosion will be totally destroyed. Even people living outside this area will be in danger from –

HEAT AND BLAST

FALL-OUT

Heat and Blast

The heat and blast are so severe that they can kill, and destroy buildings, for up to five miles from the explosion. Beyond that, there can be severe damage.

Fall-out

Fall-out is a dust that is sucked up from the ground by the explosion. It can be deadly dangerous. It rises high in the air and can be carried by the winds for hundreds of miles before falling to the ground.
The radiation from this dust is dangerous. It cannot be seen or felt. It has no smell, and it can be detected only by special instruments. Exposure to it can cause sickness and death. If the dust fell on or around your home, the radiation from it would be a danger to you and your family for many days after an explosion. Radiation can penetrate any material, but its intensity is reduced as it passes through – so the thicker and denser the material is, the better.

2 Planning for survival

Stay at Home

Your own local authority will be best able to help you in war.
If you move away – unless you have a place of your own to go to or intend to live with relatives – the authority in your new area will not help you with accommodation or food or other essentials. If you leave, your local authority may need to take your empty house for others to use. So stay at home.

Plan a Fall-out room and Inner Refuge

The first priority is to provide shelter within your home against radioactive fall-out. Your best protection is to make a fall-out room and build an inner refuge within it.

First, the Fall-out room

Because of the threat of radiation you and your family may need to live in this room for fourteen days after an attack, almost without leaving it at all. So you must make it as safe as you can, and equip it for your survival. Choose the place furthest from the outside walls and from the roof, or which has the smallest

amount of outside wall. The further you can get, within your home, from the radioactive dust that is on or around it, the safer you will be. Use the cellar or basement if there is one. Otherwise use a room, hall or passage on the ground floor.
Even the safest room in your home is not safe enough, however. You will need to block up windows in the room, and any other openings, and to make the outside walls thicker, and also to thicken the floor above you, to provide the strongest possible protection against the penetration of radiation. Thick, dense materials are the best, and bricks, concrete or building blocks, timber, boxes of earth, sand, books, and furniture might all be used.

Flats

If you live in a block of flats there are other factors to consider. If the block is five storeys high or more, do not shelter in the top two floors. Make arrangements now with your landlord for alternative shelter accommodation if you can, or with your neighbours on the lower floors, or with relatives or friends.
If your flat is in a block of four storeys or less, the basement or ground floor will give you the best protection. Central corridors on lower floors will provide good protection.

Bungalows

Bungalows and similar single-storey homes will not give much protection. Arrange to shelter with someone close by if you can do so.
If not, select a place in your home that is furthest from the roof and the outside walls, and strengthen it as has been described.

Caravans

If you live in a caravan or other similar accommodation which provides very little protection against fall-out your local authority will be able to advise you on what to do.

Now the Inner Refuge

Still greater protection is necessary in the fall-out room, particularly for the first two days and nights after an attack, when the radiation dangers could be critical. To provide this you should build an inner refuge. This too should be thick-lined with dense materials to resist the radiation, and should be built away from the outside walls.

Here are some ideas:

1. Make a 'lean-to' with sloping doors taken from rooms above or strong boards rested against an inner wall. Prevent them from slipping by fixing a length of wood along the floor. Build further protection of bags or boxes of earth or sand – or books, or even clothing – on the slope of your refuge, and more also against slipping. Partly close the two open ends with boxes of earth or sand, or heavy furniture.

2. Use tables if they are large enough to provide you all with shelter. Surround them and cover them with heavy furniture filled with sand, earth, books or clothing.

3. Use the cupboard under the stairs if it is in your fall-out room. Put bags of earth or sand on the stairs and along the wall of the cupboard. If the stairs are on an outside wall, strengthen the wall outside in the same way to a height of six feet.

PLAN YOUR SURVIVAL KIT
Five essentials for survival in your Fall-out Room

1 Drinking Water

You will need enough for the family for fourteen days. Each person should drink two pints a day – so for this you will need three and a half gallons each.
You should try to stock twice as much water as you are likely to need for drinking, so that you will have enough for washing. You are unlikely to be able to use the mains water supply after an attack – so provide your drinking water beforehand by filling bottles for use in the fall-out room. Store extra water in the bath, in basins and in other containers.
Seal or cover all you can. Anything that has had fall-out dust on it will be contaminated and dangerous to drink or to eat. You cannot remove radiation from water by boiling it.

2 Food

Stock enough food for fourteen days.
Choose foods which can be eaten cold, which keep fresh, and which are tinned or well wrapped. Keep your stocks in a closed cabinet or cupboard.
Provide variety. Stock sugar, jams or other sweet foods, cereals, biscuits, meats, vegetables, fruit and fruit juices. Children will need tinned or powdered milk, and babies their normal food as far as is possible. Eat perishable items first.
Use your supplies sparingly.

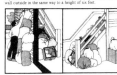

3 Portable Radio and Spare Batteries

Your radio will be your only link with the outside world. So take a spare one with you if you can.
You will need to listen for instructions about what to do after the attack and while you remain in your fall-out room.

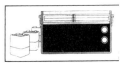

4 Tin Opener, Bottle Opener, Cutlery and Crockery

5 Warm Clothing

These further items will also be useful in the Fall-out Room:

6. Bedding, sleeping bags

7. Portable stove and fuel, saucepans

8. Torches with spare bulbs and batteries, candles, matches

9. Table and chairs

10. Toilet articles, soap, toilet rolls, bucket and plastic bags

11. Changes of clothing

12. First aid Kit – with household medicines and prescribed medicines. And at least Aspirins or Codeine tablets, adhesive dressings, cotton wool, bandages, disinfectant, ointment, including 'Vaseline'

13. Box of dry sand, cloths or tissues for wiping plates and utensils

14. Notebook and pencils for messages

15. Brushes, shovels and cleaning materials, rubber or plastic gloves, dustpan and brush

16. Toys and magazines

17. Clock (mechanical) and calendar

Here are some ideas:

1. Make a 'lean-to' with sloping doors taken from rooms above or strong boards rested against an inner wall. Prevent them from slipping by fixing a length of wood along the floor. Build further protection of bags or boxes of earth or sand – or books, or even clothing – on the slope of your refuge, and anchor these also against slipping. Partly close the two open ends with boxes of earth or sand, or heavy furniture.

At home

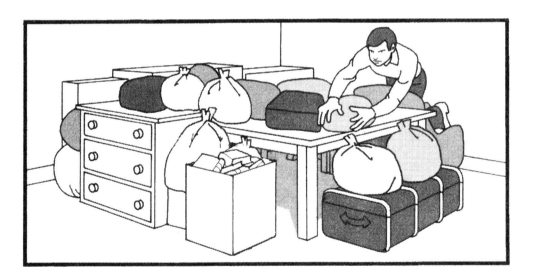

The makeshift table shelter in the initial draft of *Protect and Survive* features cushions and mattresses; the illustration was altered before publication to include bulkier items like crates of books (*above*). In the late 1990s, the iconic image of a family waiting to enter their fallout shelter (*opposite*) was repurposed by artists Stanley Donwood and Dr Tchock for the cover of the Radiohead single *Karma Police*.

Script 4

STAY AT HOME

4/1

4/2

Vision   Symbol. Fade in cloud still as inlay.   Fade out symbol and zoom in on cloud still.

Sound   *SOUND EFFECT*   *We have told you that ...*

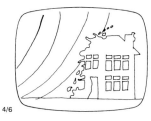

4/6

4/7

Vision   "Blast" sequence from Script 1.   Animated cloud/dust graphic.

Sound   *Blast can destroy buildings miles away from the explosion*   *Fall-out is dust that is sucked up from the ground by the explosion*

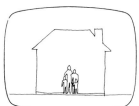

4/11

4/12

Vision   Mix to house silhouette with family group.   Animate to form ring around symbol within house.

Sound   *So you are just as safe in your own home area. In fact...*   *you are far better off at home because it is the place you know and where you are known. So stay where you are*

In other quarters, investigative journalist Duncan Campbell's revelatory book *War Plan* UK, which uncovered the shambolic state of civil defence in Britain, pointed out many of the flaws of *Protect and Survive*. The booklet inspired countless parodies from the anti-nuclear protest movement. Ben Hayden followed the government's instructions, building his own fallout shelter near a housing estate in Limehouse, and documenting his experience in *Ben's Bunker Book* – styled after the government booklet. Campaigner E. P. Thompson published a riposte on behalf of the peace movement, *Protest and Survive*, with early editions also designed to look like the official pamphlet. Newspaper ads taunting the government over the campaign were placed by the Greater London Council (GLC), and photomontage artist Peter Kennard created an iconic image of a human skeleton reading the booklet; this montage enjoyed plenty of reuse by protest groups such as CND, frequently with the caption 'Ever wish you were better informed?'. The upset was lasting: young CND members were still protesting its sale outside the government's Stationery Office bookshop in Edinburgh the following summer.

Despite this very public damage to the campaign's reputation, it was not a complete washout. By the summer of 1981, more than 80,000 copies of the revised booklet had been sold; a tape of the films, which had been loaned out to local authorities, was viewed so many times by early 1984 that it fell apart and had to be replaced. Behind the scenes, the Home Office continued to think about the future of the *Protect and Survive* advice. In August 1984, they investigated whether it could be repurposed using new technology, by preparing an electronic version aimed at the 1.6 million homes with Teletext-capable televisions, as well as the 50,000 users of British Telecom's early Prestel computer network. However, nothing seems to have come of the idea.

Opposite: A page from the original storyboards for the *Protect and Survive* films. Image from The National Archives, INF 6/2294.

Next pages: Those protesting nuclear weapons were quick to parody *Protect and Survive*.

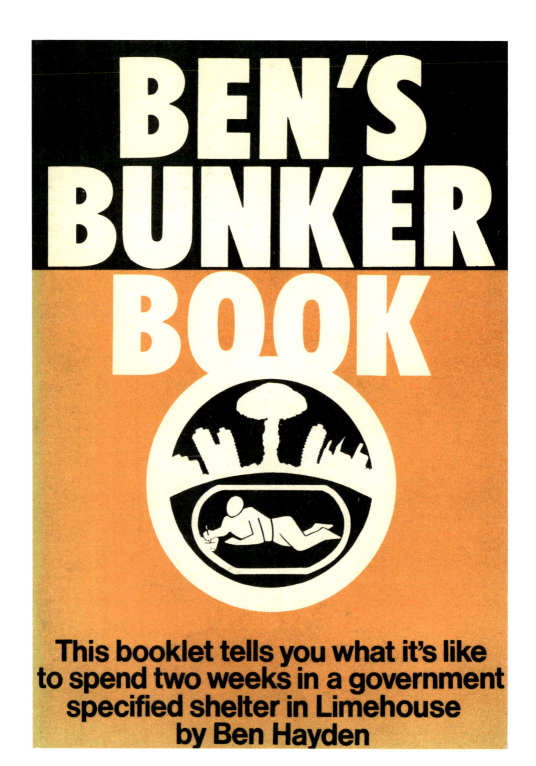

BEN'S BUNKER BOOK

This booklet tells you what it's like to spend two weeks in a government specified shelter in Limehouse by Ben Hayden

PROTEST AND SURVIVE

E. P. Thompson

Several other official publications came out under the Protect and Survive banner, taking design cues from their parent brand: *Domestic Nuclear Shelters*, *Domestic Nuclear Shelters: Technical Guidance*, and *Civil Defence: Why We Need It*.

Domestic Nuclear Shelters was an attempt to bring bunkers to the masses. Published in 1981, it was comprised of two publications – a thin A5 pamphlet, and *Domestic Nuclear Shelters: Technical Guidance*, a much more comprehensive A4 book. The former was intended as an extremely basic introduction to bunker-building for ordinary householders, while the larger volume was aimed at tradesmen, engineers, and perhaps the more dedicated or paranoid homeowner. A working group had been set up to develop the *Technical Guidance* manual, which ended up being revised and republished several times during the 1980s. This included detailed schematics of several types of shelter, with technical data on protective factors against blast and fallout. Meanwhile, the Central Office of Information worked on the slimmer *Domestic Nuclear Shelters* pamphlet. This combined shelter designs produced by the Working Group with general information about nuclear weapons, advice on what to expect during nuclear attack, and a shopping list for stocking your bunker. Intended for wider distribution, this version, like *Protect and Survive*, was priced at just 50 pence.

One of the shelters depicted in both versions of the guide, the 'Type 2' indoor shelter, is identical to the 'Morrison' shelter used in the Second World War – essentially a large metal table. The step-by-step construction diagrams are almost exactly the same as those found in a 1941 pamphlet, *How to Put Up Your Morrison 'Table' Shelter* – with the clothing simply updated from 1940s to 1980s fashions. It's tempting to think that this was a subversive act on the part of the designer.

While the chunky *Technical Guidance* book survived into the second half of the 1980s, its smaller A5 companion pamphlet did not. In early 1983, the Home Office reviewed its publications on nuclear attack, taking the decision not to publish a new edition of the pamphlet. The plan was to merge the basic shelter information into any future *Protect and Survive*-style booklet. An internal memo in 1986 described the lightweight *Domestic Nuclear Shelters* booklet as 'neither flesh nor fowl', being 'an odd mixture of superficial shelter information, descriptions of effects mixed with rationale, and *Protect and Survive*-style advice'. The option to further revise the *Technical Guidance* book was left open – albeit in a form 'in which the word 'nuclear' is used as little as possible' – but the idea of a standalone pamphlet was ditched for good.

Civil Defence: Why we need it (1981).

CIVIL DEFENCE

why we need it

Civil Defence: Why We Need It also carried the Protect and Survive branding, but this thin pamphlet didn't offer any advice. Published late in 1981 as a response to the public outcry over the government's civil defence programme, it set out to defend the government's position, in a question-and-answer format, curiously ending with the phrase 'Civil defence is common sense' – an official slogan which hadn't enjoyed currency since the mid-1960s. One final booklet, *Nuclear Weapons*, can be grouped with these; although it did not feature the *Protect and Survive* branding, it was frequently referred to alongside the others. *Nuclear Weapons* was intended for a more technical audience, and provided in-depth descriptions of the science behind nuclear weapons, their effects, and protective measures.

While the bulk of the government's advice was for city dwellers, there was some limited information available for those in the countryside. *Nuclear Weapons* detailed the potential impact on food, water, crops and livestock, and two publications were aimed specifically at farmers: *Home Defence and the Farmer* in 1958, and *Civil Defence and the Farmer* in 1985.

The public humiliation of *Protect and Survive* had a lasting effect, making governments wary of producing anything like it again. In 1986, Home Secretary Douglas Hurd said: 'If new material was issued now, everyone would throw it into the wastepaper basket or make fun of it as they did with *Protect and Survive*. I don't think there's a sensible purpose in it.' Yet, the same year, the government produced a new, lower-key campaign. Known as *Civil Protection*, the A4 booklet was a primer on the various catastrophes that might befall British citizens. Covering more than just nuclear attack, it included threats such as major industrial accidents and natural disasters like flooding. The Civil Protection campaign had virtually no public impact, mostly targeting emergency planners instead. Rather than creating a new 'brand', it adopted the international symbol for civil defence as defined by the Geneva Conventions – a blue triangle on an orange background. Detailed training materials were prepared for community volunteers, known as the Community Adviser Training Course. This was backed by colourful slides showing the flash, blast, heat and fallout involved in a nuclear attack. A series of Civil Protection videos was created, too, dealing with nuclear weapons effects, first aid, emergency feeding and the staffing of rest centres – each video echoing one of the duties that had been core to Britain's civil defence preparations since the very start. As the Cold War came to an end, the Civil Protection name lived on as a quarterly Home Office magazine for emergency planners, with its publication continuing into the early years of the new millennium.

Domestic Nuclear Shelters (1981).

DOMESTIC NUCLEAR SHELTERS

Advice on domestic shelters providing protection against nuclear explosions

A Home Office guide

Type 2
Indoor shelter from manufactured kit

This type of shelter — basically a protective steel table — is suitable for homes that have basements or rooms that can be converted into 'fallout rooms' (described in *Protect and Survive*) provided that the floor is strong enough to support it.

This shelter will sustain the debris load resulting from the complete collapse of a normal two-storey house. To obtain protection from fallout, it must be surrounded with dry-laid bricks, sand or earth bags or heavy furniture filled with sand, earth or books.

The shelter is designed to accommodate two adults and two children. Two shelters or more may be put together to increase the capacity.

It would take two people about two hours to erect the shelter itself and up to an additional 20 hours to surround it with protective material.

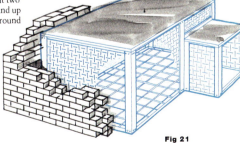

Fig 21

Plan of shelter in 'fallout room'.

13

Home Defence and the Farmer

PRICE ONE SHILLING NET

BRECONSHIRE DIVISION

HER MAJESTY'S STATIONERY OFFICE

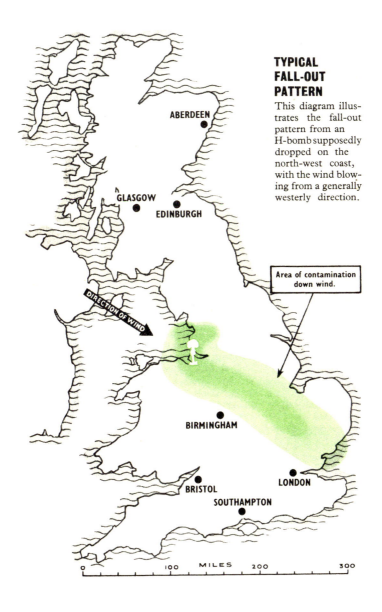

TYPICAL FALL-OUT PATTERN

This diagram illustrates the fall-out pattern from an H-bomb supposedly dropped on the north-west coast, with the wind blowing from a generally westerly direction.

ABERDEEN

GLASGOW
EDINBURGH

DIRECTION OF WIND

Area of contamination down wind.

BIRMINGHAM

BRISTOL
SOUTHAMPTON

LONDON

0   100   MILES   200   300

Home Defence and the Farmer (1958) offered basic advice to the farming community, and was part of a wider campaign which included a short film.

Next pages: The Home Office produced a set of training posters in 1958 which depicted typical British street scenes before and after a nuclear attack.

Buildings: mainly

of load bearing wall construction

Typical view of sho

Nominal bomb air burst
Damage at about
3,000 - 4,000 ft.
from G.Z.

Buildings: severe damage, most buildings beyond repair

Streets: major obstruction by debris

Direction of blast

2a

Damage at about 4 - 5 miles

m ground-burst 10 m.t. bomb (=500n)

Buildings: steel framed
and
load bearing wall construction

Typical view in centre of city   1

Buildings:
load bearing wall construction

Typical two storey domestic property   4

Nominal bomb
air burst
Damage at about ½ mile from G.Z.

Buildings: load-bearing walls destroyed, severe damage to steel framed buildings

Streets: completely blocked with debris

Direction of blast

1a

Damage at about 3-4 miles from ground-burst 10 m.t. bomb (=500n)

Nominal bomb air burst

6,000 ft. - 8,000 ft.

Buildings: damage to roofs, windows, partitions etc.

Streets: scattered with light debris

Direction of blast

4a

Damage at about 7-10 miles from ground-burst 10 m.t. bomb (=500n)

In the latter half of the 1980s, each local authority was encouraged to recruit
'community advisers' to act as expert volunteers during a transition to war,
and after attack. These course materials from 1987 included a large training folder
and a series of slides explaining nuclear weapon effects.

Effects of Radiation on People

Whole Body Doses

Normally receive about 0·1r annually
Up to 150r No acute effects. Some malaise

Above 150r Increasing sickness and incapacitation. Some mortality in 2—4 weeks

Above 350r Serious sickness and incapacitation. Heavy mortality in 2—4 weeks

Above 600r Immediate sickness and — rapid mortality

our

(radiation)

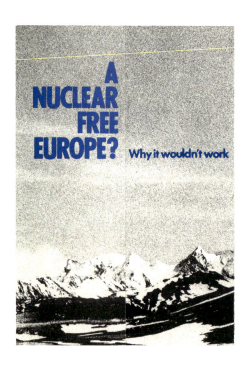

A NUCLEAR FREE EUROPE?

Why it wouldn't work

NUCLEAR WEAPONS AND PREVENTING WAR

1 Nuclear weapons have transformed our view of war. Though they have been used only twice, half a lifetime ago, the terrible experience of Hiroshima and Nagasaki must be always in our minds. But the scale of that horror makes it all the more necessary that revulsion be partnered by clear thinking. If it is not, we may find ourselves having to learn again, in the appalling school of practical experience, that abhorrence of war is no substitute for realistic plans to prevent it.

2 There can be opposing views about whether the world would be safer and more peaceful if nuclear weapons had never been invented. But that is academic; they cannot be disinvented. Our task now is to devise a system for living in peace and freedom while ensuring that nuclear weapons are never used, either to destroy or to blackmail.

3 Nuclear weapons are the dominant aspect of modern war potential. But they are not the only aspect we should

fear. Save at the very end, World War II was fought entirely with what are comfortably called "conventional" weapons, yet during its six years something like fifty million people were killed. Since 1945 "conventional" war has killed up to ten million more. The "conventional" weapons with which any East-West war would be fought today are much more powerful than those of 1939-1945; and chemical weapons are far more lethal than when they were last used widely, over sixty years ago. Action about nuclear weapons which left, or seemed to leave, the field free for non-nuclear war could be calamitous.

4 Moreover, whatever promises might have been given in peace, no alliance possessing nuclear weapons could be counted on to accept major non-nuclear defeat and conquest without using its nuclear power. Non-nuclear war between East and West is by far the likeliest road to nuclear war.

EITHER SIDE OF THE URALS - IT'S STILL TARGET EUROPE

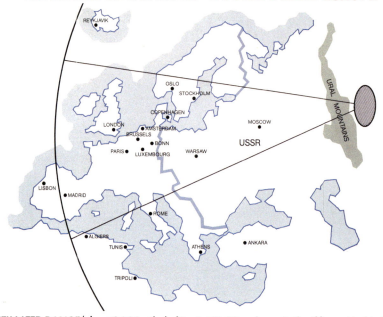

ESTIMATED RANGE (about 3,000 miles) of Soviet SS-20 nuclear missiles if based behind the Urals.

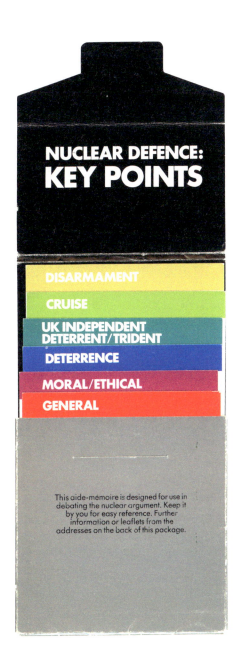

NUCLEAR DEFENCE:
KEY POINTS

DISARMAMENT

CRUISE

UK INDEPENDENT
DETERRENT/TRIDENT

DETERRENCE

MORAL/ETHICAL

GENERAL

This aide-mémoire is designed for use in
debating the nuclear argument. Keep it
by you for easy reference. Further
information or leaflets from the
addresses on the back of this package.

The Home Office was not alone in creating public information about
nuclear attack. In 1981–2, the Ministry of Defence's publicity department
issued a series of leaflets defending the nuclear deterrent, including a handy
pack of 'key points' designed to help their holder win arguments.

Both the popular and specialist media covered the threat of nuclear attack on the United Kingdom, with coverage increasing in the early 1980s. The left-leaning *Daily Mirror* devoted much of its 6 November 1980 edition to the topic, reporting on the sleepy English villages that had unwittingly become Soviet targets, the 'Four-Minute Warning' that would be issued from RAF Fylingdales, and what life would be like for the survivors. A few months later, *Time Out* magazine focused on the psychological response to the threat in an article on the 'bombshock syndrome'. It related the fears of ordinary people, such as Ellen from Sheffield, whose frequent nightmares of nuclear holocaust had been fuelled by *Protect and Survive*, mixed with memories of disaster fiction such as the BBC's post-apocalyptic drama *Survivors*. It also highlighted those cashing in on the threat – one broker of Swedish-designed fallout shelters said he hoped to be installing 500 a year by 1984.

Those who were prepared to invest in their own shelter would have found plenty to enjoy in *Protect and Survive Monthly*. Despite the name, it was not an official publication, although its first issue, in January 1981, did feature a letter of encouragement from Leon Brittan MP, the minister responsible for civil defence. With guides for prospective bunker buyers, practical advice for survival, and reports on civil defence from around the world, PSM was the go-to publication for those who wanted to act on their nuclear anxiety. Over time, it gradually became odder, with a later issue asking: 'Will your pet survive a nuclear war?'. The politics of this home-grown magazine's publishers, while always close to the surface, became increasingly transparent, too: articles began to address the 'Marxist threat', and offered advice not just on defending your home against Russian missiles, but against burglars and criminal youths, too. In 1983, *Protect and Survive Monthly* left newsstands for good, transforming into the subscriber-only *Practical Civil Defence*. This ran until early 1986, before disappearing altogether in a flurry of last-ditch appeals to subscribers for more cash.

Opposite and next pages: covers from *Protect and Survive Monthly* (1981–82) and *Practical Civil Defence* (1983).

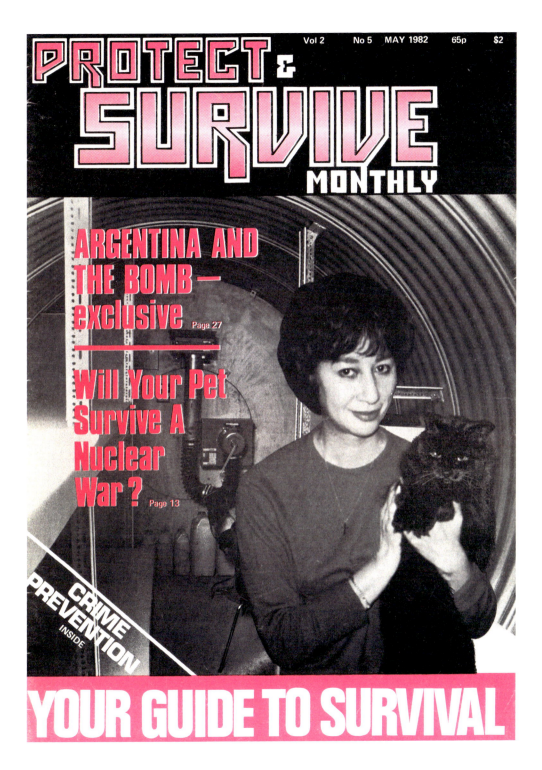

Vol 2   No 5   MAY 1982   65p $2

PROTECT & SURVIVE MONTHLY

ARGENTINA AND THE BOMB — exclusive Page 27

Will Your Pet Survive A Nuclear War? Page 13

CRIME PREVENTION INSIDE

YOUR GUIDE TO SURVIVAL

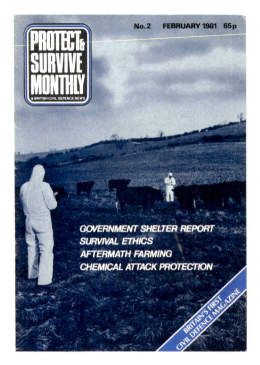

No. 2 FEBRUARY 1981 65p

PROTECT & SURVIVE MONTHLY
& BRITISH CIVIL DEFENCE NEWS

GOVERNMENT SHELTER REPORT
SURVIVAL ETHICS
AFTERMATH FARMING
CHEMICAL ATTACK PROTECTION

BRITAIN'S FIRST
CIVIL DEFENCE MAGAZINE

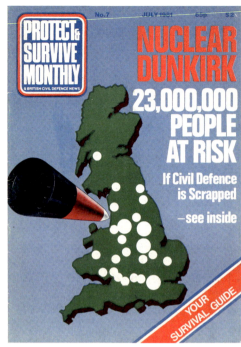

No.7 JULY 1981 65p $2

PROTECT & SURVIVE MONTHLY
& BRITISH CIVIL DEFENCE NEWS

NUCLEAR DUNKIRK

23,000,000 PEOPLE AT RISK

If Civil Defence is Scrapped

—see inside

YOUR SURVIVAL GUIDE

No.8 AUGUST 1981 65p $2

PROTECT & SURVIVE MONTHLY
& BRITISH/U.S. Civil Defence News

WAR IN SPACE
FACT OR FICTION?

INTERNATIONAL SURVIVAL GUIDE

Ken Barendale

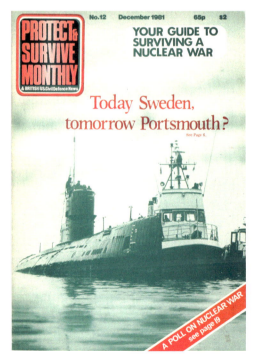

No.12 December 1981 65p $2

PROTECT & SURVIVE MONTHLY
& BRITISH/U.S. Civil Defence News

YOUR GUIDE TO SURVIVING A NUCLEAR WAR

Today Sweden, tomorrow Portsmouth?

See Page 6.

A POLL ON NUCLEAR WAR
see page 19

Practical

CIVIL DEFENCE

JULY/AUGUST 1983 Bi-Monthly

Subscriptions UK & Eire £18
— Canada & USA $38
— Rest of World £25

"Civil Defence is a humanitarian ideal –
It seeks to save lives and alleviate
suffering in time of war,
natural disaster and
man-made accidents."

CHEMICAL WARFARE
ARE WE PREPARED?

see pages 11 - 29

A cottage industry in private nuclear bunkers and fallout shelters developed in the early 1980s. Most of these were small spaces designed to be installed in a back garden, and would have offered few home comforts beyond a bed and a washing area; however, with a built-in generator and air filtering system, they did give you some significant advantages over the basic lean-to described in *Protect and Survive*. Whether there would be any advantage in being a survivor is another question.

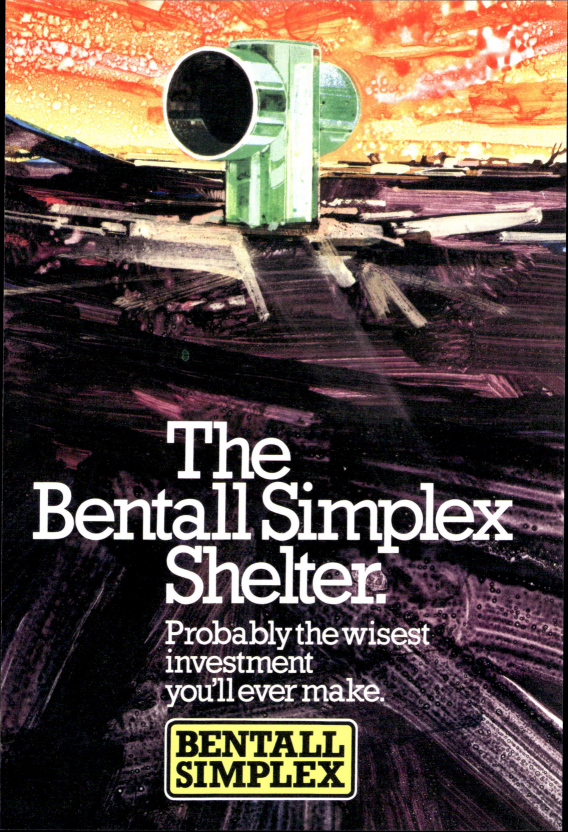

An unusual alternative to the garden shelter was the Project Eastlays scheme. With prices starting at £2,000 per person, families could lease an 'apartment' deep below the Wiltshire countryside. The mysterious company behind the project, Rusepalm Ltd, claimed that Eastlays quarry, a former government ammunitions dump, would be converted into some 2,500 apartments, creating an underground city of up to 10,000 people. In May 1981, local MP Richard Needham called Rusepalm 'speculators' in Parliament and questioned whether their name was 'a hidden pun on the confidence trick that the company may be attempting to play on the ordinary public, or on the fact that the Russians may attack us'. The company collapsed soon afterwards, without having made any progress.

The early 1980s saw a growing number of companies
of varying levels of trustworthiness offering worried members
of the public their own nuclear shelters.

Getting Involved

Britain's readiness for nuclear attack spread far beyond the corridors of central government. The opportunities to get involved in preparing for the unthinkable were wide-ranging: several volunteer organisations owed their existence to the threat of the Bomb; others found that it intruded on their professional duties; and, for a few, it was the focus of their job.

Civil Defence recruitment was a big deal in the 1960s; this campaign guide offered a variety of booklets, leaflets, posters and films which could be ordered to help entice new volunteers to join.

CIVIL DEFENCE CAMPAIGN GUIDE

recruitment & publicity 1962

The UK's first national-scale volunteer recruitment for civil defence duties had taken place in the build-up to the Second World War. The government called on the public to become Air Raid Precautions (ARP) wardens, fire spotters, rescuers and first aiders, and to look after those injured or made homeless by air attacks. As the war in Europe drew to an end, the ARP organisation – by then known as the Civil Defence (General) Services – was stood down from duty. But as relations with Stalin's Soviet Union deteriorated, the Civil Defence Act 1948 called for the reinstatement of a national civil defence organisation. The following year, the Civil Defence Corps was founded, recruiting volunteers to train for similar duties to those in wartime – wardens, rescuers, first aiders, and people to provide welfare services, such as food and rest centres. This time round, though, there was a new threat; on 23 September 1949, the future of the Civil Defence Corps was cemented as the US announced that the Soviet Union had detonated their first atomic bomb.

Despite wearing military-style uniforms, the Civil Defence Corps was run as a civilian volunteer organisation, open to men and women. Overall authority lay with the Home Office, but day-to-day operations were devolved to the 'Corps Authorities' run by local councils. Throughout the 1950s and 1960s, Civil Defence Corps volunteers took part in regular exercises simulating major disasters in their local areas, including nuclear attack. Recruitment materials emphasised not only the value people could bring to the organisation by volunteering, but the opportunity it provided for self-development. They commonly featured phrases like 'Civil Defence is common sense'; 'Millions could survive'; 'Use the best in you'; 'Your abilities will be fully used' and 'Civil Defence is people plus'. Recruitment leaned heavily on the social aspect of joining up, featuring photographs of volunteers relaxing, dancing, and playing darts and table tennis. The Civil Defence Corps continued to train until 1968, when, following a cost-cutting government review, it was permanently axed.

Opposite and next pages: The late 1950s and early 1960s saw a flurry of publicity designed to recruit men and women to the Civil Defence Corps. Designs moved with the times, with wartime imagery gradually being replaced by pared-back layouts featuring bold typography.

WHY
CIVIL
DEFENCE
NEEDS
PEOPLE
LIKE

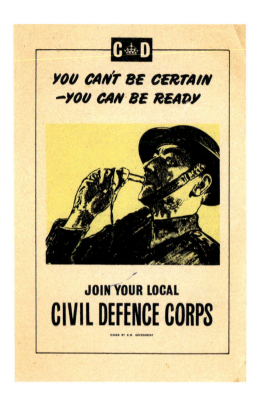

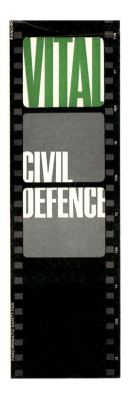

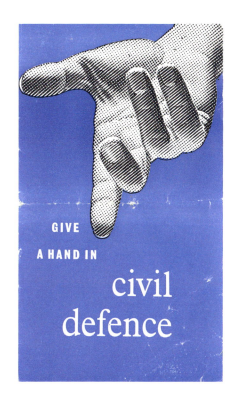

GIVE
A HAND IN
civil
defence

THE H-BOMB
What about the millions of survivors?

CIVIL DEFENCE
is common sense

USE
THE
BEST
IN
YOU

here in Civil Defence

TODAY'S
CIVIL DEFENCE

Lives of whole neighbourhoods would depend upon planned

BOMB BURST

MEAN WIND

INHABITANTS MUST
BE EVACUATED
AFTER 48 HRS

NORMAL LIVING
POSSIBLE AFTER
48 HRS

TIME TO BE SPENT IN THE
OPEN MUST BE
LIMITED FOR SOME WEEKS

The mushroom cloud of an H-bomb takes with it thousands of tons of earth and debris in the form of dust which has been made radioactive through contact with the fireball. When this dust, or fall-out as it is called, settles again, it will be giving off radiations which are harmful to the human body. *Where* it falls depends upon the weather and in particular the wind. Fortunately these radiations lose their potency with time—the radioactivity of the dust 'decays'. In two days the fall-out would be one hundred times less dangerous than at first—which isn't to say that it wouldn't still be harmful to life. You can withstand a high degree of radiation for a short time, and a lower degree of radiation for a correspondingly longer time. But the effect builds up and there is a limit to the total amount the body can survive.

OUTER
WALL

SANDBAGGED
WINDOW

GROUND FLOOR ROOM WITH
ONE OUTER WALL

Today's Civil Defence (early 1960s).

There's time to relax . . . and for making new friends

. . . in Civil Defence

THE SOCIAL SIDE . . .

Dances, socials, get-togethers, darts matches, whist drives, table tennis or just sitting back, after the evening's training, with a cup of tea, a cigarette and a few good friends . . . you'll enjoy yourself in Civil Defence as much as these people here.

Today
willingness to help
is not enough —

Be <u>able</u> to help

JOIN
CIVIL
DEFENCE

Prepared by the Central Office of Information for H.M. Government.   H.O. 6114

Printed for H.M. Stationery Office by Petty & Sons Ltd. 51-5641

PERCENTAGE CASUALTIES FROM GROUND
BURST MEGATON BOMBS (ALL IN HOUSES, NEGLECTING EFFECTS OF FALL OUT)

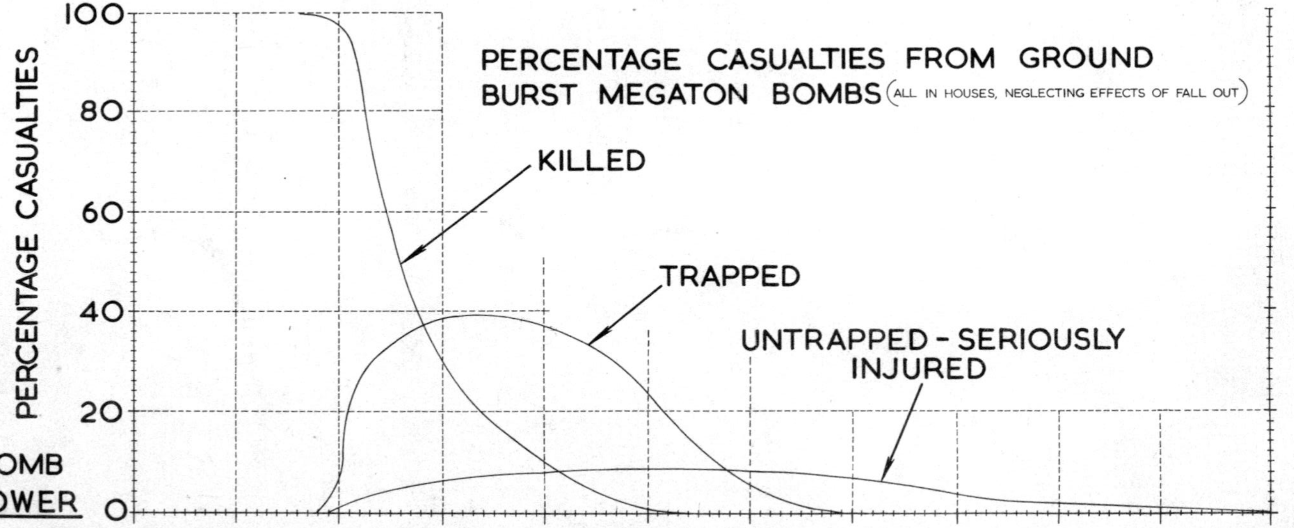

KILLED

TRAPPED

UNTRAPPED - SERIOUSLY INJURED

PERCENTAGE CASUALTIES

100 — 80 — 60 — 40 — 20 — 0

BOMB POWER	1	2	3	4	5	6	7	8	9	10	11
10 MT	0·8	1·6	2·4	3·2	4·0	4·8	5·6	6·3	7·1	7·9	8·7
5 MT	0·6	1·2	1·8	2·3	2·9	3·5	4·1	4·7	5·3	5·9	6·4
2 MT	0·5	0·9	1·4	1·9	2·3	2·8	3·3	3·7	4·2	4·7	5·1
1 MT	0·4	0·7	1·1	1·5	1·8	2·2	2·6	2·9	3·3	3·7	4·1
½ MT	0										

DISTANCE FROM G.Z. (MILES)

By permission of the Controller of H.M.S.O.

Ref. 9·4·B

GREVILLES PHOTOGRAPHIC SERVICES LTD. Trading Estate, Slough

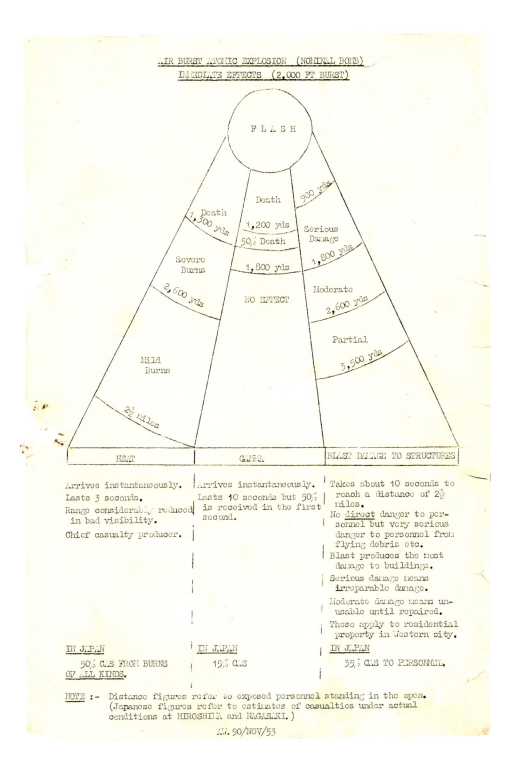

AIR BURST ATOMIC EXPLOSION (NOMINAL BOMB)
IMMEDIATE EFFECTS (2,000 FT BURST)

FLASH

Death
1,300 yds

Death
900 yds

Death
1,200 yds

50% Death

Serious
Damage

Severe
Burns

1,800 yds

2,600 yds

1,800 yds

Moderate

NO EFFECT

2,600 yds

Partial

Mild
Burns

3,500 yds

2½ miles

HEAT	GAMMA	BLAST DAMAGE TO STRUCTURES
Arrives instantaneously. Lasts 3 seconds. Range considerably reduced in bad visibility. Chief casualty producer.	Arrives instantaneously. Lasts 10 seconds but 50% is received in the first second.	Takes about 10 seconds to reach a distance of 2½ miles. No direct danger to personnel but very serious danger to personnel from flying debris etc. Blast produces the most damage to buildings. Serious damage means irreparable damage. Moderate damage means unusable until repaired. These apply to residential property in Western city.
IN JAPAN 50% CAS FROM BURNS OF ALL KINDS.	IN JAPAN 15% CAS	IN JAPAN 35% CAS TO PERSONNEL.

NOTE :- Distance figures refer to exposed personnel standing in the open.
        (Japanese figures refer to estimates of casualties under actual
        conditions at HIROSHIMA and NAGASAKI.)

AM.90/NOV/53

Fallout Prediction Template

Previous pages: Training materials used by members
of the Civil Defence Corps ranged from professionally-produced
exercises to hand-typed information.

Look at the diagram below and write in the appropriate box GZ, the upwind distance, the plume and the hot line. Compare your completed diagram with the one on the next page.

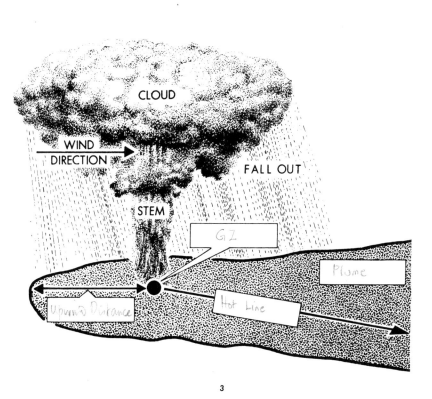

CLOUD

WIND DIRECTION

FALL OUT

STEM

GZ

Plume

Upwind Distance

Hot Line

3

Above and opposite: The government's Home Defence College
at Easingwold issued training materials for emergency planners, including,
in 1978, the *Fallout Prediction Template* exercise book.

The Royal Observer Corps (ROC) was a civilian volunteer force, founded in 1925 as the Observer Corps, and tasked with watching the skies for incoming air raids. In 1941, they were granted the prefix 'Royal' in recognition of their contribution to the Battle of Britain. In 1955, following the Strath Report, the government instituted 'a national monitoring organisation to give warning and to measure radioactivity in the event of air attack' – the United Kingdom Warning and Monitoring Organisation (UKWMO), to whom the ROC would report. This added a key new task to the ROC's duties: the volunteers, known as 'observers', would now be trained to report the direction and power of nuclear strikes.

During regular training and exercises, observers crewed tiny, three-person bunkers, known as ROC posts, which were constructed on a grid system across the United Kingdom. A spate of government bunker-building led to more than 1,500 posts being constructed by 1968, stretching from the Lizard at the southern tip of Cornwall to Voe in the north of Shetland's Mainland. Each post was equipped at surface level with a ground zero indicator (GZI) to determine the location of a nuclear explosion, a bomb power indicator (BPI) to measure its force, and a fixed survey meter (FSM) to detect and measure fallout. Below ground, posts were fitted with a 'Teletalk' loudspeaker telephone, which allowed observers to report the information they gathered about nuclear blasts back to their group control, who would pass the information on to the UKWMO.

...and you're among friends in to

'I like the
sense of
responsibility
...'

'It gets you
out of a rut
...'

'Everyone's
so friendly
...'

'You le
new sk

Like the Civil Defence Corps, the social aspect of the ROC was a big draw; as well as training and spending hours together in posts, members would attend annual camps in each other's company, leading to many lasting friendships being formed. The bulk of the ROC's activity was ended as the Cold War drew to a close in 1991. Some posts were abandoned and left to decay; others were ploughed over by the farmers on whose land they had been constructed. Others still were later rescued and restored by dedicated volunteers – many of whom had themselves served in the ROC. Some observers expressed an interest in continuing to lend their expertise at Regional Government Headquarters (RGHQ) bunkers – huge, multi-level sites that the government had initially intended to keep open after the Cold War ended. However, in January 1993 the hopeful volunteers were let down: a line was drawn under the programme, and the RGHQs were sold off (those at Anstruther in Fife, Hack Green in Cheshire and Kelvedon Hatch in Essex were subsequently transformed into successful visitor attractions). Former observers received personal letters announcing the decision from the Head of UKWMO, while Home Secretary Kenneth Clarke MP wrote to warning point operators to thank them for their service. A small part of the Royal Observer Corps was kept alive in the form of the Nuclear Reporting Cells, which reported directly to the RAF. Their specialist nuclear burst and fallout prediction skills were retained until the end of 1995, at which point the ROC's story officially came to an end.

's Royal Observer Corps

'...meet people from all walks of life.'

'The social life is so active...'

'You really feel you *belong*...'

'It certainly *is* different...'

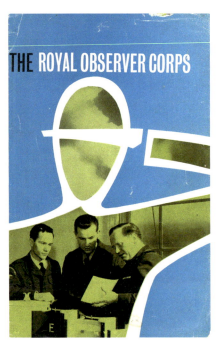

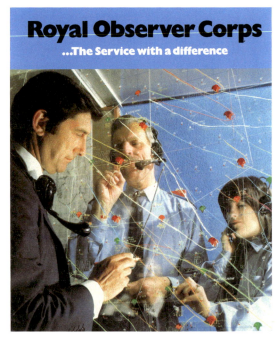

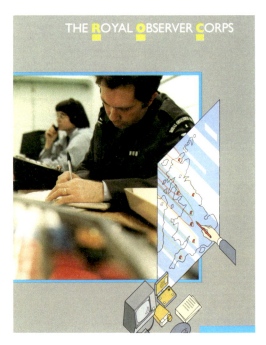

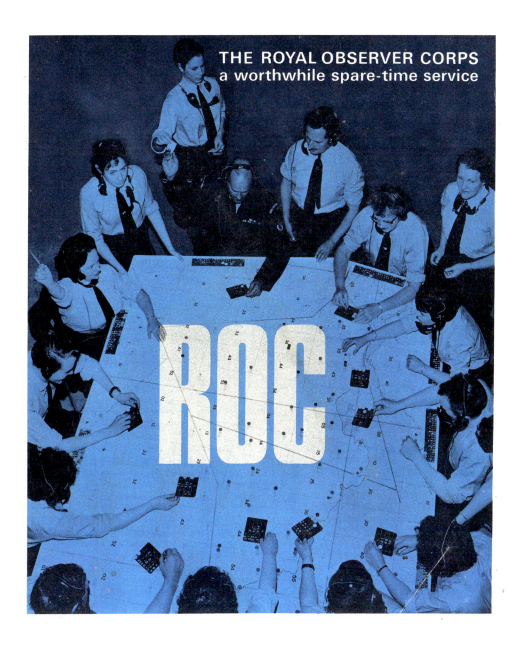

THE ROYAL OBSERVER CORPS
a worthwhile spare-time service

Like the Civil Defence Corps, the Royal Observer Corps produced recruitment materials which combined the idea of 'worthwhile service' with the opportunity for a broader social circle. In the 1970s and 1980s, these predominantly took the form of large, colourful fold-out brochures showing Observers at work.

ROYAL OBSERVER CORPS

Overleaf: Pages from Post Personnel Training Scheme materials
prepared for the Royal Observer Corps (1989).

ROYAL
OBSERVER
CORPS

RETIRE FROM MAROON

TAKE COVER

FIREBALL ACTION
and CLOUD FORMATION

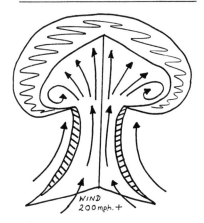

WIND
200mph. +

The Fireball rises leaving a partial vacuum and air flows in from the surrounding area to fill it.

A FEW OBSERVERS
WILL SUFFER FROM
SEVERE
STRESS

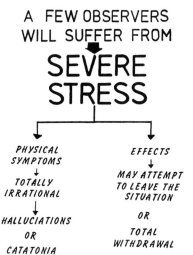

PHYSICAL SYMPTOMS
↓
TOTALLY IRRATIONAL
↓
HALLUCIATIONS OR CATATONIA

EFFECTS
↓
MAY ATTEMPT TO LEAVE THE SITUATION

OR

TOTAL WITHDRAWAL

WIND SPEED 13 KNOTS

DUST AND PAPER SWIRL SMALL BRANCHES MOVE

MEDIUM BREEZE

WIND SPEED 30 KNOTS

WHOLE TREES MOVE

HIGH WIND

WIND SPEED 52 KNOTS

TREES UPROOTED STRUCTURAL DAMAGE

WHOLE GALE

WIND SPEED 60 KNOTS

WIDESPREAD DAMAGE

STORM

The Women's Voluntary Services (WVS) was founded in 1938, and grew to over a million members during the Second World War, assisting with evacuation, distributing clothing, providing food and drink and generally helping those in need. After the war, the WVS took on a new role as part of the Civil Defence apparatus, providing welfare services for the Civil Defence Corps, such as organising convoys to feed huge numbers of people during a crisis. They also focused on educating women about the threat posed by the Bomb through the 'One-in-Five' scheme – the name coming from their goal of speaking to a fifth of women across the country. Specially-trained, Home Office-approved speakers would visit groups of women in church halls, factories, offices, and even their own homes, to explain how they could practically mitigate the effects of nuclear attack. In 1966, the organisation became known as the Women's Royal Voluntary Service (WRVS), and, outliving the other civil defence organisations, continues its community work today as the Royal Voluntary Service, albeit without the nuclear education aspect.

Opposite and overleaf: Promotional literature produced for the WVS (and later WRVS) One-in-Five scheme aimed to recruit a fifth of Britain's women to learn about the atomic threat.

What has the fifth heard
that the other four haven't ?

The WVS One-in-Five Talks
of course

These talks give you, in an interesting form, the facts about possible effects of a nuclear explosion and what you could do to protect your family, your home and yourself.

More information from your W.V.S. Centre.

Issued by: Women's Voluntary Service for Civil Defence, 41 Tothill Street, London, S.W.1

OF.6

Wt. 35243/374 500m. 10.59 We. & S. Gp. 362.

SURVIVAL!

We all want to prevent nuclear war.
But, if it ever came, we would all have to know the do's and don'ts that could help many families to survive. This series of five diagrams explains the facts about our protection in the survival areas.

OF 11   PREPARED FOR THE W.V.S. BY THE CENTRAL OFFICE OF INFORMATION

INDICATIONS OF DANGER

BEFORE ATTACK

FIRST STAGE
There would be an official instruction to take precautions.

SECOND STAGE
Our warning system is designed to provide a warning before an attack reaches this country, giving enough time to get under cover.

DURING ATTACK

The light from a nuclear explosion would warn those not under cover to seek instant protection against the other possible dangers – heat, blast, radio-active fall-out.

AFTER ATTACK

Warnings would be given to those places which fall-out was approaching.

The United Kingdom Warning and Monitoring Organisation (UKWMO) was a civilian organisation which employed thousands of trained staff, the majority of whom were spare-time volunteers. The UKWMO's role was to issue warnings of nuclear attack and fallout, confirm nuclear strikes, liaise with NATO countries on nuclear bursts, and provide technical data about any attack to the UK government and military forces. During an attack, staff would collate reports from the Royal Observer Corps in order to tri-angulate the precise position of each nuclear burst, calculate its power, and the direction of fallout, as well as issue meteorological reports.

Operating with a skeleton staff during peacetime, including a small group of full-time employees at Cowley Barracks in Oxfordshire, the UKWMO claimed it could become fully-operational in a matter of hours during a period of rising international tension. They would have been responsible for issuing Britain's infamous 'four-minute warning'. Notice of incoming missiles would come from the Ballistic Missile Early Warning System (BMEWS), a complex system connecting the 'golf ball' radomes at RAF Fylingdales in Yorkshire with similar stations at Thule, Greenland and Clear, Alaska. The UKWMO could broadcast the warning to 250 warning carrier control points, located within major police stations. At the push of a button, the police could then remotely activate their local warning sirens, of which there were around 7,000 in total. Rural areas were home to a further 11,000 warning points, found in police, fire and coastguard stations, civil and military establishments, hospitals, industrial centres, and – where there was nowhere more suitable – in shops, pubs and private houses. These were controlled by designated warning point operators, who would alert local residents using a hand-cranked siren or by firing maroons (loud rockets) on receiving the signal. The four-minute warning relied on the public being aware of how to act on hearing the sirens, which is where the broad distribution of public information such as *Protect and Survive* would be vital in the weeks leading up to a nuclear strike.

The UKWMO's structure, and role in warning the nation, are outlined
in these promotional booklets from 1974 (pages 91–93) and 1985 (pages 94–95).

09 57 hrs Fylingdales, Yorkshire: radar detects an attack on this country. The United Kingdom Warning and Monitoring Organisation acts immediately. Its job is to warn the public.

UKWMO

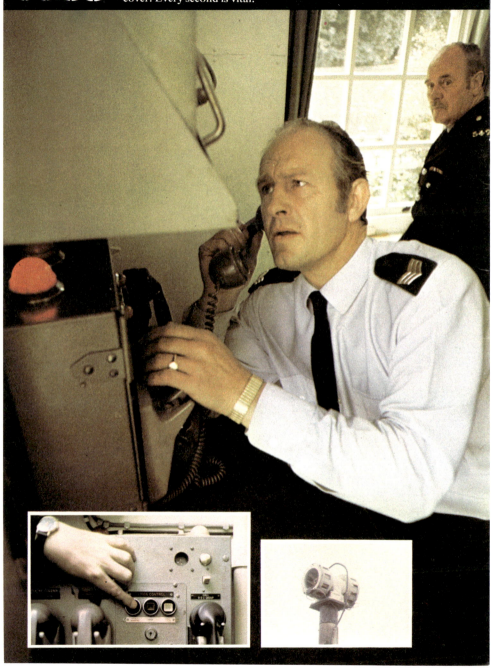

0958 Enemy attack warning received by 250 carrier control points in major police stations. Police sound sirens – warning public to take cover. Every second is vital.

1003

Underground monitoring posts also register nuclear explosions. Information is passed to Group Controls in minutes or even seconds. *Inset:* Surface view of one post.

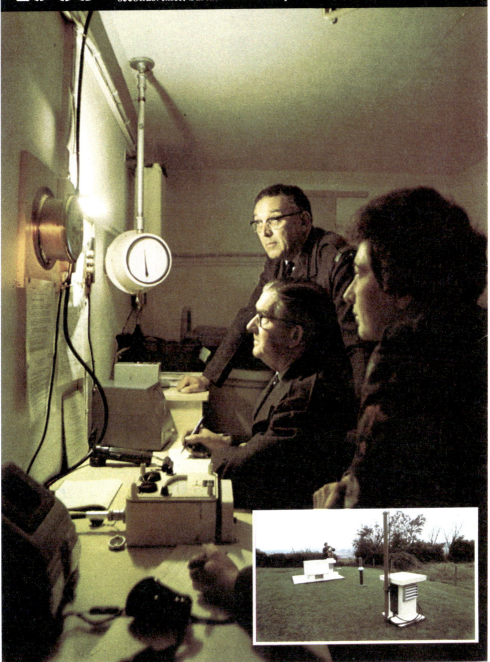

UKWMO

UNITED KINGDOM WARNING AND MONITORING ORGANISATION

SECTOR CONTROL ...

1 The Sector Operations Room

2 Assessing the radiological situation

3 Maintaining a national picture of bomb bursts and the threat they pose

4 Defining the area covered by fallout from each bomb burst

8

Police

The police's role was not simply to turn on sirens; had Britain been attacked with nuclear weapons, they would have had vital duties to carry out in order to maintain law, order and the continuation of the state. These were detailed in an evolving series of guides, intended for internal use, issued by the Home Office and the Scottish Home and Health Department.

The first of these, the *Police War Duties Manual*, was issued in 1966. A pocketable guide to police responsibilities in wartime, it described tasks after attack such as monitoring fallout with Radiac survey meters; restoring law, order and 'public morale'; controlling traffic; guarding key installations; helping the homeless get to rest centres, and handing over prisoners of war to the military. When the prospect of nuclear war was looming, a significant segment of serving police – 40 per cent in some areas – would be pulled from duty and organised into 'mobile columns': self-supporting units who would carry everything they needed to survive for a week. These could then be deployed to where they were needed most.

An updated version was published in 1974 as the *Police Manual of Home Defence*, and again as *Guidance to the Police Service on War Emergency Planning* in 1985. This final edition added a short, new section, titled Administration of Justice, addressing a topic which its predecessors had studiously managed to avoid. 'In the aftermath of a widespread nuclear attack,' it said, 'There would inevitably be a period during which the present machinery of justice would not be fully effective... Surviving members of the judiciary would be expected to organise their resources to re-establish a fair and civilised judicial system commanding the confidence of the surviving population... Penalties and the treatment of offenders would be a matter for the government of the day, in the circumstances of the time.'

Police Manual of Home Defence (1974) gave guidance for police forces on their pre- and post-attack role.

SCOTTISH HOME AND HEALTH DEPARTMENT

Police Manual of Home Defence (Scotland)

Copies will be sold only on written application by Chief Constables to Her Majesty's Stationery Office

Restricted

Edinburgh Her Majesty's Stationery Office

40p net

The General Post Office (GPO) was responsible both for the postal service and telecommunications across the United Kingdom until 1981, when British Telecom was spun off into an independent organisation. It was therefore vital that Post Office staff were prepared for the Bomb.

Employees who had been assigned a wartime duty were issued with a slim *War Emergency Instructions* booklet. It read: 'In the event of a nuclear attack, the Post Office would have the vital task of providing essential communications upon which life-saving operations would depend. Thereafter, the means of support for the many millions who had survived would also rely heavily on our services.'

The Post Office was responsible for key communication centres, including secret underground bunkers at London (known as KINGSWAY), Birmingham (ANCHOR) and Manchester (GUARDIAN). These deep-level telephone exchanges were located among city centre shops and office buildings, with plain-looking surface-level buildings designed not to attract attention. As well as these major installations, the GPO was also responsible for many more sites around the country, including a national line-of-sight microwave communications network, whose most prominent tower was the GPO (BT) Tower in London. The booklet issued to staff continued: 'You have been assigned a task at one such location. After arrival, you must not leave that location without authority. You will imperil your own life and the vital communications upon which the survival of our families and the nation depends if you do.'

Selected Post Office workers in the early 1970s
were issued with a slim guide to their wartime duties.

POST OFFICE
WAR EMERGENCY INSTRUCTIONS

RADIATION SAFETY

Advice to Post Office Staff performing Essential Tasks

Naturally, the armed forces would play a significant role in defending the United Kingdom during a war. But, in the event of a nuclear attack, those stationed in Britain would be as much at risk as the public. To that end, they were issued with instructions on how to react: a 1978 manual, *Army NBC Survival in the United Kingdom*, was supplemented by a pocket-sized laminated card, *Nuclear Survival in the UK*, which combined the Army's own advice with segments lifted directly from *Protect and Survive*. Illustrations from the public information manual are reproduced wholesale, with the ordinary householder simply replaced by a drawing of a soldier.

Army NBC Survival in the United Kingdom (1978).

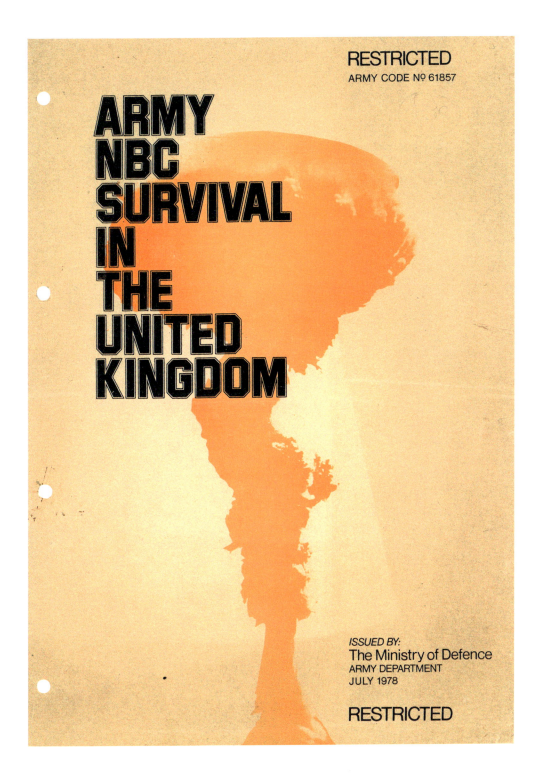

ARMY
NBC
SURVIVAL
IN
THE
UNITED
KINGDOM

ISSUED BY:
The Ministry of Defence
ARMY DEPARTMENT
JULY 1978

Local Authorities

Central government intended that local authorities across the country should play a leading role in preparing for nuclear attack. Some were proactive and enthusiastic supporters of civil defence, while many more – for a variety of political, ideological and practical reasons – made no effort to disguise their contempt for the programme.

In peacetime, the UK government imposed a number of requirements on local councils to prepare for nuclear attack, via the Civil Defence Regulations. They required councils to appoint Emergency Planning Officers (EPOs), whose responsibilities included the preparation of a 'war plan' for their area. Each council had to maintain two bunkers – a main one, and a standby; they had to be actively working on updating their civil defence plans, and they had to be willing to take part in national civil defence exercises. Controversial changes to the regulations in 1983 gave ministers powers to order the councils to comply. This was because some, mainly left-leaning, local authorities were ideologically opposed to civil defence; with the growth of the Nuclear Free Zones movement in the early 1980s, some councils essentially opted out of fulfilling all but the bare minimum activities required to comply with the letter of the law.

Had a nuclear attack occurred, a swathe of legal responsibilities awaited local authorities. They were supposed to advise the public on protective measures; identify potential shelters, provide rest centres, first aid and emergency feeding facilities; bury the dead; prevent disease from spreading, and maintain transport links and essential services. Obliged to create war plans to provide a framework for life after a nuclear attack, emergency planning departments created what became known as 'war books'. Distributed strictly to those who needed to see them, each war book set out a council's plan for post-apocalyptic governance – usually in the form of a ring binder that could be easily and periodically updated.

Councils on the right of the political spectrum were enthusiastic authors of war books. Wiltshire County Council's *War Emergency Guide Book*, compiled between 1966 and 1979, sought to provide guidance on everything from preventing disease to monitoring fallout. However, the bulk of the advice and training material it contained was around

MERSEYSIDE
AND THE BOMB
40p

103

maintaining order. During a 'transition to war' period, counties would switch to being directly governed by a controller, often the council's chief executive, who would find themselves with significant power over their local area. In Wiltshire, official guidance said that 'law and order should be enforced by *ad hoc* methods under arrangements by controllers. Justice may have to be administered by summary courts... punishments will probably be corporal and immediate.' 'It is desirable that the armed services should be responsible for the execution of sentences,' it continued. 'Firm action in the early stages may prevent the situation getting out of hand.' Training exercises for community advisers posed scenarios involving the council quelling food riots and apprehending violent looters, and asked questions like: 'Can I order a man to be executed?' and 'Where do I stand if there is ever an investigation?'

Charged with preparing emergency public information (to be issued where the distribution of guides like *Protect and Survive* was impossible), local authorities created basic leaflets that could be printed up as a double-sided A4 sheet, and therefore easily reproduced *en masse* using a council photocopier. Cornwall County Council's 'local information sheet – wartime crisis' included crudely hand-drawn diagrams showing the effects of nuclear weapons, and the local government chain of control in an emergency.

Whether or not they toed the official line around civil defence, local authorities were not shy about producing their own public information materials on the theme of nuclear attack. A surprisingly large number of local, and sometimes hyper-local, official guides were produced in the early 1980s that envisaged the effects of nuclear attack on their areas, and – depending on the political standpoint of the council – either piled on anxiety or tried to provide reassurance. Those councils which opposed the Conservative government frequently played up the local destruction a nuclear attack would cause, and underlined the pointlessness, in their view, of civil defence. In the absence of a sufficiently major local target, such as an RAF base, radar station or ammunition depot, the hypothetical – and improbable – Soviet missile targets in these booklets would be the town hall or another landmark familiar to local people. Those that did support the aims of civil defence were themselves frustrated at times: when the first edition of *Protect and Survive* was released in 1976, its distribution was prohibited. This led to some councils repackaging parts of the official guidance in their own booklets for their local residents, with varying degrees of success, sometimes combined with outdated advice from older government booklets.

Gwent And Emergency Planning (1983).

GWENT

AND EMERGENCY PLANNING

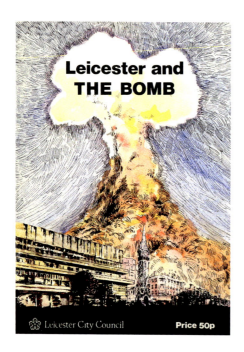
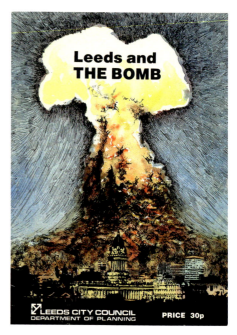

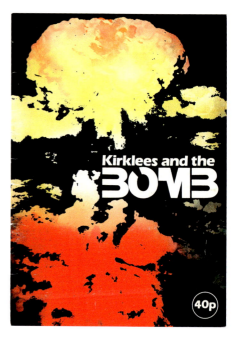

This page: Various *...and the Bomb* booklets (1983–84).
Opposite and next pages: *Hull and the Bomb* (1983).

HULL and the BOMB

50p

The Effects of a One Meg Bomb on Queen's Garde

TOTAL PROBABLE CASUALTIES

262,000 out of the City's population of 268,000 could be killed or injured.

BLAST DAMAGE

Black rings

Within 1.75 miles:
All buildings destroyed;
98% killed.

Within 2.8 miles:
Most buildings destroyed;
50% killed, 40% injured.

Within 4.8 miles:
Buildings severely damaged;
5% killed, 45% injured.

HEAT DAMAGE

Red circles

Within 5 miles:
3rd degree and fatal burns in the open. Most buildings on fire. Possible fire-storm.

Within 6 miles:
2nd degree burns (bad blistering) in the open.

Within 7 miles:
1st degree burns in the open.

RADIO-ACTIVE FALL-OUT

Grey shaded areas.

Survivors of heat and blast would receive lethal doses of radiation within 2 days.

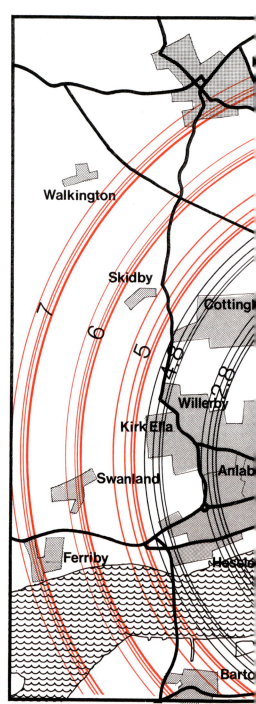

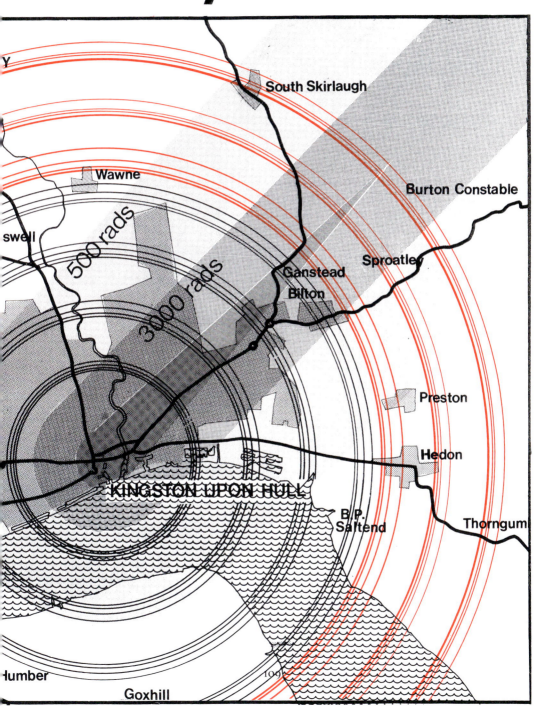

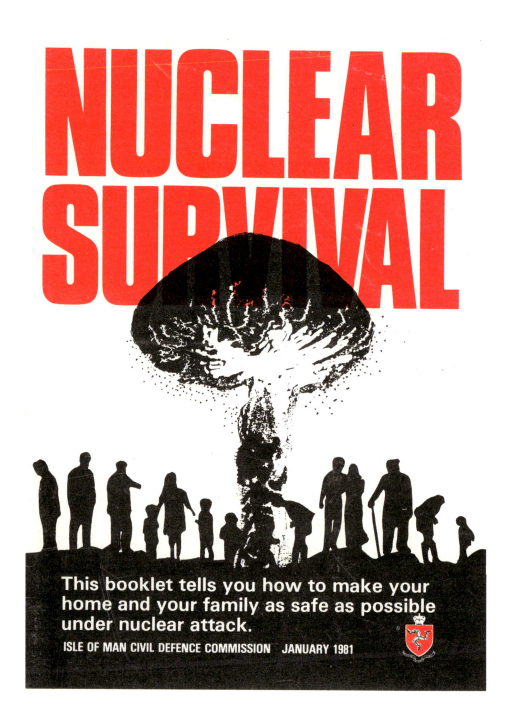

Nuclear Survival, Isle Of Man Civil Defence Commission (1981).

Protect & Survive?, Harlow District Council (1983).

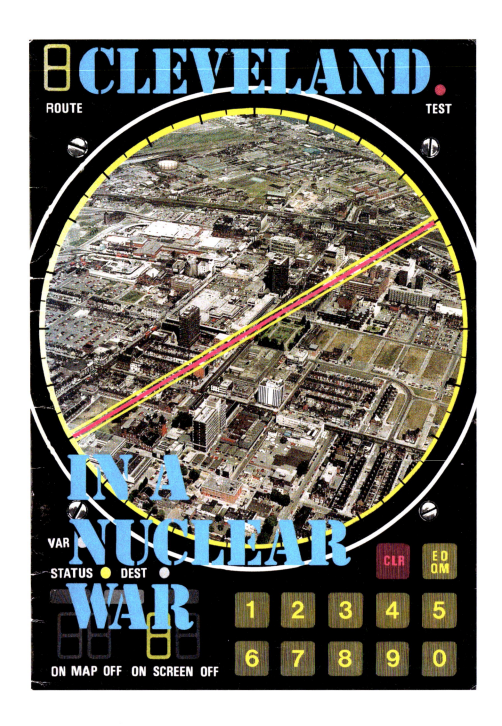

Cleveland in a Nuclear War, Cleveland County Council (1983).

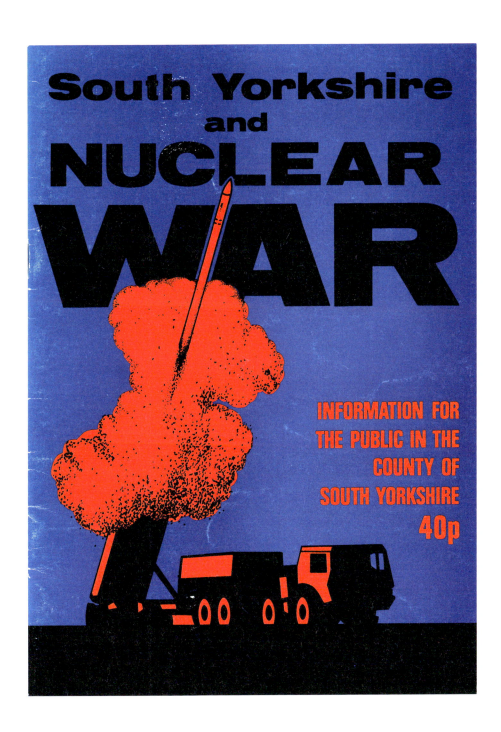

South Yorkshire and Nuclear War, South Yorkshire County Council (1984).

COUNTY OF AVON

HOUSEHOLDER'S GUIDE TO SURVIVAL IN NUCLEAR WAR

March 1980

Householder's Guide to Survival in Nuclear War, County of Avon (1980).

Householder's Survival Guide, Hingham Parish Council (1982).

1 MEGATON GROUNDBURST NUCL
at Lime Street Station

CASUALTIES – 375,000 killed or injured
out of population of 500,000

BLAST DAMAGE

**78,000 killed
1,500 injured
All buildings destroyed**

**55,000 killed
43,000 injured
Most buildings destroyed**

**8,000 killed
80,000 injured
Buildings severely damaged**

HEAT EFFECTS

third degree or fatal burns

second degree or serious burns

first degree or mild burns

RADIO-ACTIVE FALLOUT
(south westerly wind)

■ ■ ■ fallout contours

400-600 rads = lethal
155,000 survivors could
receive this dose in 2 days

HO

WEST

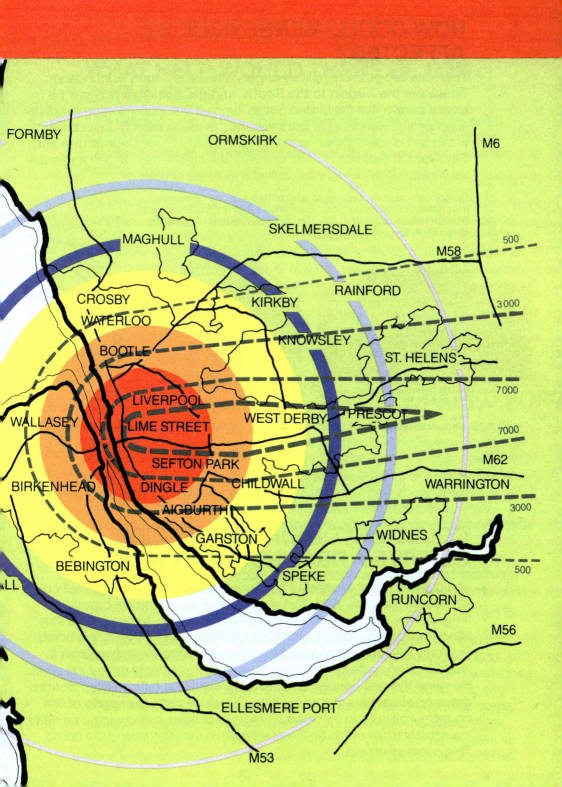

Lincolnshire

WILL TO SURVIVE

A guide to basic protection in the event of nuclear attack

Published by
Lincolnshire County Council
County Offices
Lincoln LN1 1YL

CORNWALL COUNTY COUNCIL

EMERGENCY PLANNING SECTION TRURO

LOCAL INFORMATION SHEET - WARTIME CRISIS

****

The Civil Defence (General L.A. Functions) Regulations(1983) place a statutory duty o Greater London Council and the County Councils of England and Wales, to make plans for providing and maintaining a range of local services essential to the life of the community in the event of a hostile attack upon this Country (that is either conventional or nuclear war).

****

At local level, Parishes/Towns etc. have been asked to form emergency committees and to do some basic planning tasks for their community. Some committees cater for both civil and wartime emergencies.

****

This pamphlet is intended as information to individuals in the event of a national wartime crisis. For details contact your local Parish/Town Council or Area Emergency Planning Officer. Telephone.

- -

Previous page: This graphic from *Merseyside and the Bomb* detailed the impact of a one-megaton warhead on Liverpool.

This page: Publications from Linconshire and Cornwall.

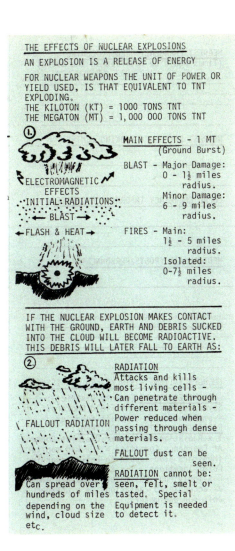

THE EFFECTS OF NUCLEAR EXPLOSIONS

AN EXPLOSION IS A RELEASE OF ENERGY

FOR NUCLEAR WEAPONS THE UNIT OF POWER OR YIELD USED, IS THAT EQUIVALENT TO TNT EXPLODING.
THE KILOTON (KT) = 1000 TONS TNT
THE MEGATON (MT) = 1,000 000 TONS TNT

(1.)

ELECTROMAGNETIC
EFFECTS
INITIAL RADIATIONS
← BLAST →
← FLASH & HEAT →

MAIN EFFECTS - 1 MT
(Ground Burst)

BLAST - Major Damage:
0 - 1½ miles
radius.
Minor Damage:
6 - 9 miles
radius.

FIRES - Main:
1½ - 5 miles
radius.
Isolated:
0-7½ miles
radius.

IF THE NUCLEAR EXPLOSION MAKES CONTACT WITH THE GROUND, EARTH AND DEBRIS SUCKED INTO THE CLOUD WILL BECOME RADIOACTIVE. THIS DEBRIS WILL LATER FALL TO EARTH AS:

(2.)

FALLOUT RADIATION

Can spread over hundreds of miles depending on the wind, cloud size etc.

RADIATION
Attacks and kills most living cells -
Can penetrate through different materials -
Power reduced when passing through dense materials.

FALLOUT dust can be seen.
RADIATION cannot be: seen, felt, smelt or tasted. Special Equipment is needed to detect it.

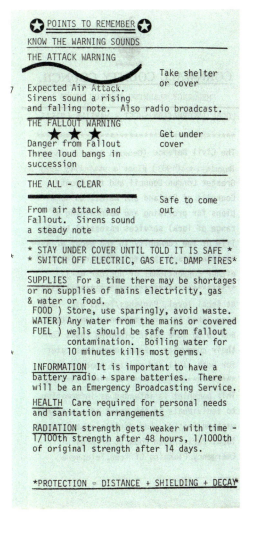

★ POINTS TO REMEMBER ★

KNOW THE WARNING SOUNDS

THE ATTACK WARNING

Take shelter
or cover

Expected Air Attack.
Sirens sound a rising and falling note. Also radio broadcast.

THE FALLOUT WARNING

★ ★ ★

Get under cover

Danger from Fallout
Three loud bangs in succession

THE ALL - CLEAR

Safe to come out

From air attack and Fallout. Sirens sound a steady note

* STAY UNDER COVER UNTIL TOLD IT IS SAFE *
* SWITCH OFF ELECTRIC, GAS ETC. DAMP FIRES *

SUPPLIES For a time there may be shortages or no supplies of mains electricity, gas & water or food.
FOOD) Store, use sparingly, avoid waste.
WATER) Any water from the mains or covered
FUEL) wells should be safe from fallout contamination. Boiling water for 10 minutes kills most germs.

INFORMATION It is important to have a battery radio + spare batteries. There will be an Emergency Broadcasting Service.

HEALTH Care required for personal needs and sanitation arrangements

RADIATION strength gets weaker with time - 1/100th strength after 48 hours, 1/1000th of original strength after 14 days.

PROTECTION = DISTANCE + SHIELDING + DECAY

Overleaf: Wiltshire County Council's war book set out
the stages of the expected lengthy pre-attack period.

Ups   and   downs   of   everyday   life

GROUP I – Action by Community Adviser Alone

1

2

3

4

5

GROUP II – Action Involving Certain Key Peopl

1

2

3

4

5

GROUP III – Action Under the Auspices of the

1

2

3

4

5

A potentially dangerous situation

Preoccupation with crisis news and
television

Serious note sounded by commentators

Anxiety and apprehension displayed
by public

Crisis meetings by government

Comment by Ministers

Reaction by public

Serious reaction by
public indicating break-
down in order, supply,
communications, etc.

rship

Covert warning

Overt warning

 STRIKE

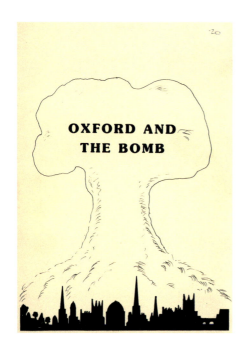
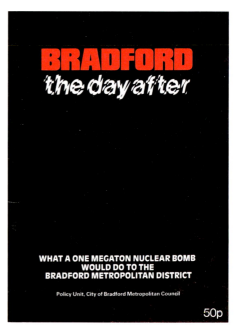
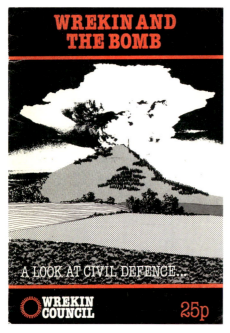

Publications from Oxford (1984), Bradford (1984),
Wrekin (1984) and West Sussex (1979).

WARPLAN BRIGHTON

The truth about local civil defence

Surviving the Bomb – how to look after yourself and your family

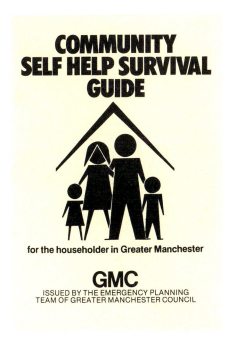

COMMUNITY SELF HELP SURVIVAL GUIDE

for the householder in Greater Manchester

GMC

ISSUED BY THE EMERGENCY PLANNING
TEAM OF GREATER MANCHESTER COUNCIL

London as a Nuclear Free Zone

GLC
Working for London and Peace

Publications from Brighton (1983), West Yorkshire (1980),
Manchester (1981) and London (1985).

"On hearing you may resume

TO FIND OUT MORE ON WHY THE GLC'S VIEW ON CIVIL
Room 613, Greater London Counc

Material produced by the left-wing GLC's Nuclear Policy Unit outdid
most other councils, both in terms of volume and of production quality.
Their 1985 *London and Civil Defence Fact Pack* contained maps, posters
and booklets explaining why their stance was at odds with the government's.

e all-clear...
ormal activities."

(Page 24, 'Protect & Survive'. The Home Office)

DIFFERS FROM THE GOVERNMENT'S, WRITE TO:–
Block, County Hall, London SE1

KEEP THIS IN

A SAFE PLACE

YOU MAY NEED IT!

50p (One copy issued free to each householder in the Hingham Parish Area).

Author's Note

This book is not intended to be a comprehensive guide to British civil defence in the Cold War. If you are interested in learning more, I recommend the following sources.

For general insight into British civil defence and preparations for nuclear war:
Bob Clarke, *Four Minute Warning: Britain's Cold War*. Tempus Publishing, 2005
Duncan Campbell, *War Plan UK*. Paladin, 1983
Jonathan Hogg, *British Nuclear Culture*. Bloomsbury, 2016

For more on the role of the Royal Observer Corps:
Mark Dalton, *The Royal Observer Corps Underground Monitoring Posts*. Folly Books, 2017
Derek Wood, *Attack Warning Red* (2nd Edition). Carmichael and Sweet, 1992

For the architecture and infrastructure of the Cold War:
Wayne Cocroft and Roger Thomas, *Cold War: Building for Nuclear Confrontation 1946–1989*. English Heritage, 2004
Nick McCamley, *Cold War Secret Nuclear Bunkers*. Leo Cooper, 2002

Subterranea Britannica, an organisation devoted to man-made underground spaces, also takes a keen interest in nuclear bunkers, Cold War planning and civil defence in general: www.subbrit.org.uk

Finally, you can find more articles and materials on my blog at www.coldwar.org.uk

Acknowledgements

Thanks to the researchers, enthusiasts and academics who have supported my research: Danny Birchall, Dr Becky Alexis-Martin, Mike Kenner, Prof John Preston, Alistair McCann, Dr Jacquelyn Arnold, Nicholas Gould, Dr Luke Bennett, Dr Nick Blackbourn, Graham Thompson and Kevin Hall. Thanks also to my friends for their encouragement: Dave Clarke, Isobel Maclean, Sarah Gore, Catriona Melton, Caroline Kubala, Graham Taylor, Tom Snow, Dr Amy Burge and Greg Tyler; and to my parents for their continued support and patience.
Finally, thanks to Elinor Jansz and Richard Embray at Four Corners Books for making this book happen.

Opposite: Hingham Parish Council (1982).

Four Corners Irregulars
A series of books presenting a visual
history of modern British culture.
This is book 7.

Titles include:
1. Eyeball Cards, the Art
   of British CB Radio Culture
2. UFO Drawings From
   The National Archives
3. Poster Workshop 1968–1971
4. Leeds Postcards
5. Face In The Crowd
6. Wobbly Sounds, a Collection
   of British Flexidiscs

...with further volumes in preparation.

Set in Starling and printed
on Garda Matt Art Ultra.

Published in 2019 by Four Corners Books
56 Artillery Lane, London E1 7LS

This volume © Four Corners Books 2019

Designed by John Morgan Studio
morganstudio.co.uk

Print production by Martin Lee
Reprography by Flavio Milani
Printed in Italy by Printer Trento

Distributed in the UK by Art Data
artdata.co.uk

ISBN 978-1-909829-16-9

Take refuge at
fourcornersbooks.co.uk